THE
CIVIL WAR
IN COASTAL NORTH CAROLINA

THE
CIVIL WAR
IN COASTAL NORTH CAROLINA

John S. Carbone

RALEIGH
Office of Archives and History
North Carolina Department of Cultural Resources

Published with special assistance from the Outer Banks History Center

NORTH CAROLINA DEPARTMENT
OF CULTURAL RESOURCES
Lisbeth C. Evans, *Secretary*

OFFICE OF ARCHIVES AND HISTORY
Jeffrey J. Crow, *Deputy Secretary*

DIVISION OF HISTORICAL RESOURCES
David L. S. Brook, *Director*

HISTORICAL PUBLICATIONS SECTION
Donna E. Kelly, *Administrator*

Printed by PBM Graphics Inc.

www.ncpublications.com

FRONTISPIECE: These two soldiers were among the many U.S. troops that captured and occupied much of coastal North Carolina during the Civil War. The pen-and-ink drawings are by Edwin G. Champney, a Union soldier from Massachusetts who sketched numerous scenes of the Tar Heel coast during the war. The Champney Collection is located at the Outer Banks History Center, Manteo, North Carolina.

To Daniel Stephen Carbone and Suzanne Marie Carbone

Contents

Foreword

Very few topics captivate readers of North Carolina history more than accounts of the Civil War and stories about the Tar Heel coast. Now, the Historical Publications Section is pleased to combine these two fascinating subjects in *The Civil War in Coastal North Carolina*. From the drama of blockade-running to descriptions of the bloody battles that occurred in the ports and on the islands and sounds of North Carolina, the book paints a concise and explosive portrait of the events that took place in the coastal region during the great sectional conflict that changed the state and nation forever.

The author of *The Civil War in Coastal North Carolina* is John S. Carbone, M.D., a native of Hudson County, New Jersey. Although a psychiatrist by profession, Dr. Carbone has long held an enthusiasm for the history of the American Civil War, and his passion for the subject is reflected in this work. He earned his B.A. degree in history (Phi Beta Kappa) from the College of William and Mary in 1984. He graduated from the University of Virginia Medical School in 1988 and remained there through 1992 for a residency in general psychiatry, with a special emphasis on forensic psychiatry. His current position is with the Department of Corrections Hospital in Marion, Virginia, and he lives with his family in Bristol, Tennessee. Dr. Carbone has published book reviews related to Civil War history in the *North Carolina Historical Review*, and he is a member of both the Sons of Confederate Veterans and the Sons of Union Veterans.

For special assistance in publishing *The Civil War in Coastal North Carolina*, the Historical Publications Section acknowledges the staff and Associates of the Outer Banks History Center (OBHC) in Manteo, North Carolina. The OBHC, which is part of the Archives and Records Section, Office of Archives and History, provided numerous illustrations from the Edwin Graves Champney Collection of Civil War drawings, engravings, and maps for use in this volume.

Lisa D. Bailey, an editor with the Historical Publications Section, proof-read the drafts and page proofs. Mac McGee, a contract employee for the section, prepared the index. Joe A. Mobley, former administrator of the section, contributed immeasurably to this work through his editorial skill and his knowledge of both the Civil War and the North Carolina coast. He chose many of the illustrations that literally bring the book to life.

Donna Kelly, *Administrator*
Historical Publications Section

Acknowledgments

I wish to acknowledge several persons whose advice, assistance, and encouragement helped make this book possible. I am particularly grateful to Dr. Ludwell Johnson, an eminent historian and now professor emeritus at the College of William and Mary. During my undergraduate days at that institution, Dr. Johnson instilled in me a love of history that has persisted to the present, and for that I will always be grateful to him.

I also extend my thanks to Ruth and John Coski at the Eleanor S. Brockenbrough Library at the Museum of the Confederacy in Richmond, who were most helpful in ferreting out sources in the library's vast holdings. The Reverend Rachelle Kadow, a childhood friend, kindly furnished me accommodations on my research trips to Richmond. Wynne Dough, former curator, and Sarah Downing, archivist, of the Outer Banks History Center in Manteo, North Carolina, proved valuable and patient in their assistance and advice. Al and Susan Awtrey of Nags Head were kind enough to allow me to stay at their motel during a research foray to the Outer Banks, even though their facility was closed for the season. Mauriel Joslyn, an accomplished Civil War author in her own right, provided me with supportive words and the benefit of her own experience in publishing. Joe A. Mobley, former administrator of the Historical Publications Section of the North Carolina Office of Archives and History, saw potential in my writing and encouraged me to undertake this project. The photographic skills of Francene Hollander are warmly acknowledged for the flattering photo on the back cover. The medical director at my hospital in Marion, Virginia, Colin Angliker, M.D., was most accommodating in granting me leave time to travel and write.

Needless to say, without the support of my parents, Ralph Carbone, M.D., and Jean Gove Carbone, R.N., and my wife Elizabeth Carbone, R.N., M.S.W., this work would have been infinitely more difficult and less satisfying. The book is dedicated to my children, Daniel Stephen Carbone and Suzanne Marie Carbone. I hope, more than anything, that as they grow, they can come to love history and find it a source of immeasurable pleasure and fascination as I have over the years.

John S. Carbone, M.D.

The blockade-runner Banshee (the first of two vessels by that name)
made fourteen trips through the Federal blockade before being captured
in November 1863. Photograph of painting from *Official Records of the
Union and Confederate Navies in the War of the Rebellion*. Ser. 1, 9:
following 318.

PROLOGUE: *Banshee!*

One moonless night in early May 1863, a sleek gray vessel cast off from the harbor of Nassau in the Bahama Islands and, riding low to the waves, headed out of port in a northwesterly direction. Though she carried some commercially available goods, she was by no means an ordinary vessel. She was named *Banshee* (the first of two ships by that name) and was of a class of vessels designed and built for the sole purpose of evading the Federal naval blockade and supplying the Confederacy with much needed goods and war materials. The American Civil War had been raging since the spring of 1861, and blockade-runners like the *Banshee* were proving vital to keeping the Confederate States of America alive.

On this particular trip, the *Banshee* sailed for the coast of North Carolina, where she intended to slip past the U.S. blockade and discharge her cargo at the port of Wilmington, located near the mouth of the Cape Fear River. The vessel was filled to her gunwales with arms, gunpowder, anthracite coal, boots, blankets, medicine, and all manner of vital contraband of war. The ship steamed along the inlets and waterways of the Bahamian chain for as long as possible, always searching for cover and maintaining a low profile before initiating a dash for the North Carolina coastline.

The port of Wilmington offered several advantages over other possible destinations on the Confederate coast. It was near the Bahamas, where the blockade-runners took on their cargoes. Equally important was the geography of the approaches to Wilmington. Off the mouth of the Cape Fear, and jutting out into the ocean, lay Smith's Island and Frying Pan Shoals. Those obstacles obligated the Federal blockading squadron to guard the two separated channels thus forming a wide arc. These two entrances gave the blockade-runners two possibilities for running the U.S. Navy gauntlet and were "a source of major frustration for the Federal blockaders." The entrances to Wilmington were heavily fortified by a number of forts, the most formidable of which was Fort Fisher. In fact, with the exception of Charleston, South Carolina, Wilmington was considered "the most heavily fortified city on the Atlantic seaboard."

The *Banshee* encountered no trouble for her first two days out of Nassau. But when she arrived off the coast of North Carolina, Capt. Jonathan Steele, an Englishman, and the Wilmington pilot, Tom Burroughs, had to determine how to bring the ship into the mouth of the Cape Fear River, one-half mile wide, while still under the cover of near total darkness. To be caught running the gauntlet of Federal blockaders as dawn's first rays peered over the horizon spelled disaster, as a number of previous Confederate blockade-runners had already learned.

A favored technique of seasoned runners was to head twenty or more miles north of the river, thus avoiding the northernmost reach of the ring of blockaders, then turn and run along the coast southward, hugging the breakers and hoping to slip inside the cordon of U.S. vessels and gain the protection of the cannons of Fort Fisher that guarded the mouth of the Cape Fear.

On the evening that the Banshee arrived off Wilmington, the night was dark but unnervingly clear and calm. No lights were allowed on deck, including seemingly innocuous lighted cigars. Only essential crew were topside, dressed in dark clothes with their faces and hands smeared with soot, to blend with the blackness of the sky and horizon and the gray of the ship's hull. The hatches to the engine room below were covered with tarpaulins to prevent any show of light from below deck. Grimy, sweating stokers and firemen shoveled coal into the furnaces, seemingly impervious to the heat and humidity, which were magnified by the tarpaulins over the hatches.

The captain and the pilot stood on the deck while the steersman peered into the covered binnacle, trying as best he could to discern the compass needle in the almost imperceptible glow that was afforded him from the small covered lamp. After steaming for what seemed an eternity, the captain climbed to the wheelhouse and pulled a lever that rang a bell in the engine room, ordering the engineers to stop the engines so that a sounding could be taken. Stopping the ship, while necessary for a sounding, was always risky, because steam could suddenly blow off the idled engines, betraying the position with a piercing whistle for miles around. Fortunately for the Banshee, no such calamity occurred on that night. Leadsmen then took to the port and starboard chains and performed a sounding. They announced: "Nine fathoms, Captain, with a sandy bottom and black specks."

The captain acknowledged the report, and the pilot commented that the ship remained too far to the south to head toward shore. The Banshee, he said, had to be further to the north before it would be safe to attempt to turn west toward the beach and make a run south along the surf. Accordingly, the blockade-runner continued on its course for another hour before stopping again for another sounding. This time, satisfied with the location, the pilot authorized a turn toward the beach, and the captain ordered, "to port, and go ahead easy."

The *Banshee* turned and began its course southward, hugging the beach. The coastline ahead had few if any landmarks or lights to assist her. The ship stayed as close to the breakers as she dared, and several times a faint bump was felt through the hull as the vessel, riding the swelling ocean, made contact with the sandy bottom.

Shortly one of the lookouts, in a loud whisper, alerted the captain that a long, low black object lay off the port bow, perfectly silent and still. The captain took the watch's telescope and peered into the darkness. At first, he saw nothing. Slowly, however, a faint almost invisible form appeared. All aboard the *Banshee* held their collective breath as their ship glided past a darkened Federal blockader. They watched anxiously for signs of pursuit, which did not come, as the Federal vessel gradually disappeared off the port stern into the darkness. The Confederate crew sighted several more dark U.S. ships in the ensuing minutes, but the *Banshee* passed them all without being noticed.

As the blockade-runner continued on its southward course, a lookout suddenly exclaimed, "starboard, I see the Big Hill!" The hill that he sighted was a hillock as high as a full-grown oak tree. On a flat and featureless stretch of coastline it stood as a prominent and easily discerned landmark. Daylight was about to break, but the Big Hill indicated to all aboard the *Banshee* that the protection of Fort Fisher's guns was not far away. The ship poured forth as much steam and speed as she could muster. Her crew could see half a dozen Federal cruisers lying out to sea, out of range of Fort Fisher's monstrous Columbiads. Suddenly the Federal fleet fired several flares, which scorched the sky and illuminated the ocean surface and the beach in an eerie luminescence like midday. The *Banshee* had been sighted. At least two of the Federal ships must have anticipated action during the night and had kept a full head of steam. They immediately gave chase to the *Banshee*, lobbing shells at the blockade-runner from their bow chaser guns.

One of the U.S. ships fell behind in the chase, but the smaller of the two picked up speed and closed the gap with the *Banshee*. At this point, a less-experienced captain might have jettisoned cargo to lighten the load and improve speed to evade the pursuers, but that proved unnecessary. For as the blockade-runner neared Fort Fisher, the fort's artillery fired a tremendous blast at the U.S. ships in pursuit. The nearest Federal cruiser fired a parting salvo, banked sharply, and made for safer waters out of range of the fort's guns.

As the *Banshee* continued on course, the North Breaker Shoal compelled it to haul offshore and steam further out as it approached the inlet, but unfortunately for the Federals not far enough out to be within the range of their guns nor outside the protection of Fort Fisher's artillery. Then within a half hour, as daylight came to the North Carolina coast, the *Banshee* was safely over the bar and heading upriver to Wilmington. Her voyage would eventually take its place among the many exciting episodes that occurred on the coast of North Carolina during the Civil War.

Introduction

Much of North Carolina's history has been shaped by the state's unique coastline, which extends southward from the Virginia border for 300 miles until it reaches the South Carolina line. Just below 36 degrees, 30 minutes, a chain of sandbanks diverge from the mainland and continue southward for approximately 200 miles. These deposits of sand are known as the Outer Banks. They extend as far as Cape Lookout and Bogue Banks where they again approach the mainland, but not before jutting miles eastward at Cape Hatteras to the Gulf Stream, whose warm waters skirt past the cape as they travel northward before turning to cross the Atlantic Ocean.

The collision of the warm Gulf Stream with the cold southward-bound Labrador Current has created the violent storms that over the years have wrecked so many ships in the "Graveyard of the Atlantic" off Hatteras. The most famous Civil War vessel to sink off the Outer Banks was the Union ironclad *Monitor* that sank in a storm near Hatteras in December 1862. The U.S. Navy had been towing the *Monitor* to Charleston Harbor, South Carolina, for operations there when she went down in 220 feet of water.

On the Outer Banks, subtropical grasses—tolerant of the sandy soil, salt spray, and violent winds of the harsh environment—thrive along shifting sand dunes interspersed with areas of more substantial flora, such as pines, oaks, and cedars. For centuries, as weather and currents have changed (often with tremendous violence), inlets have opened and closed along the chain of barrier islands. Between the Outer Banks and the mainland of North Carolina are the sounds: Albemarle, Pamlico, Currituck, Croatan, Roanoke, Core, and Bogue. The Outer Banks created these shallow bodies of water by forming a barrier between the mainland and the ocean. Waters from various rivers—the Roanoke, the Chowan, the Pasquotank, the Alligator, the Tar-Pamlico, and the Neuse—empty into the sounds. At the outbreak of the Civil War, only five freely navigable inlets existed on the Outer Banks. From north to south, those were Oregon Inlet, New Inlet, Hatteras Inlet, Ocracoke Inlet, and Beaufort Inlet. With the exception of New Inlet, all of those remain open today.

Below the point at which the Outer Banks terminate near Cape Lookout, another series of sand islands, reefs, and small inlets stretches for the rest of the one hundred miles of coastline to the major port of Wilmington, marked by the treacherous Cape Fear and Frying Pan Shoals. There at Wilmington—North Carolina's only "deep-water port" that remained opened to the virtual end of the Civil War (a fact that played a significant role during the war)—the Cape Fear River empties directly into the ocean, the sole river within the state to do so. Despite the natural "deep-water" advantage that Wilmington enjoyed, the dangerous shoals and the violence of the weather at the cape made entry into the port precarious. During the Civil War, pilots who guided vessels into the port needed considerable navigational skill.

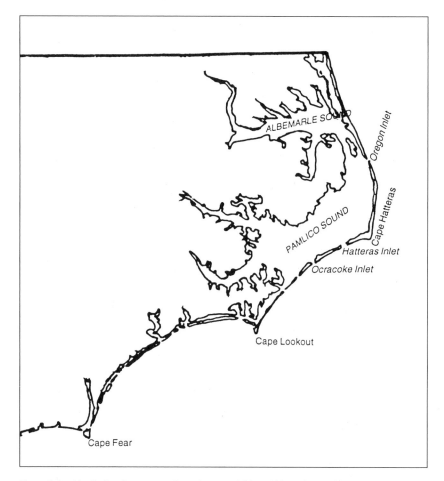

Map of the North Carolina coast. From Joe A. Mobley, *Ship Ashore! The U.S. Lifesavers of Coastal North Carolina* (Raleigh: Division of Archives and History, Department of Cultural Resources, 1994), 3.

The mainland portion of coastal North Carolina is the tidewater region of the state's Coastal Plain. The Coastal Plain consists of the area that extends inland from 100 to 150 miles from the Atlantic Ocean to the fall line of the North Carolina rivers. The tidewater is the eastern-most segment of the Coastal Plain, and it stretches from thirty to eighty miles inland on the mainland side of the sounds. Much of the tidewater contains swamps and pocosins, especially near the sounds.

Because of the peculiar geographical configuration of North Carolina's coast, created by the presence of the Outer Banks, the state, prior to the Civil War, failed to develop a large commercial economy. The shallow waters of the inlets and sounds, caused by the accumulated silt and sand trapped by the Banks, were not suitable for deep-draught shipping commerce. North Carolina never enjoyed the broad, safe, deep-water harbors that brought activity and wealth into the ports of Charleston in South Carolina and the Chesapeake Bay in Virginia. That lack of commercial development led to the state's reputation as the "Rip Van Winkle State"—namely, backward, lethargic, and culturally void.

During the first half of the nineteenth century the state made attempts to bolster its economic circumstances by improving transportation along its coast. In the late eighteenth century North Carolina and Virginia had agreed to connect their coastal regions by digging the Dismal Swamp Canal. Opened in 1828, the canal connected the Pasquotank River in North Carolina with the Elizabeth River in Virginia, but its narrow locks limited shipping and most of the trade went to Norfolk. (Today, the Intracoastal Waterway flows through the canal.) North Carolina also invested $350,000 in the Albemarle and Chesapeake Canal, which was authorized by the Virginia legislature in 1855 and intended to connect the Albemarle, Currituck, and Pamlico Sounds with the Chesapeake Bay. The canal was completed in 1859 but came under Federal control during the Civil War. The Clubfoot and Harlowe Canal, which opened around 1827, connected the Neuse River with Beaufort, but a lack of water and poor construction hindered its operations. By the time of the war, it had fallen into considerable disrepair.

Antebellum North Carolina stood high in the nation in the production of many agricultural commodities including honey, oats, rye, hay, wheat, sweet potatoes, Irish potatoes, tobacco, rice, corn, wool, hogs, cattle, and cotton. It also had a productive commercial fishing industry on the coast that in 1860 sold $120,000 worth of herring, shad, oysters, bluefish, and

The Outer Banks and sound region of the North Carolina coast.
Map from R. U. Johnson and C. C. Buel, eds., *Battles and Leaders of
the Civil War* (New York: Century Co., 1988), 4:629.

Introduction

other seafood. North Carolina possessed 639 mills that produced flour and meal, 39 cotton mills, 9 woolen mills, and 330 sawmills producing lumber. A number of facilities on the coast manufactured salt. But the state's chief economic mainstay was the naval stores industry, which derived from the massive numbers of pine trees that abounded in the Coastal Plain, particularly in the region along the Cape Fear River. From the resinous juices of the pines, workers produced the naval stores tar, pitch, and turpentine. More than fifteen hundred distilleries yielded over 65 percent of the entire prewar output of turpentine produced in the United States.

In 1859 the crop of corn in North Carolina totaled 300 million bushels, produced in eighty-four of the state's eighty-six counties, only nine of which had production of less than 200,000 bushels. In the last months of the war, this bounty fed over half of Gen. Robert E. Lee's Army of Northern Virginia in the trenches of Petersburg and Richmond. It is also a testament to the Old North State that its soldiers were probably the best supplied of the Confederacy; in April 1865, 40,000 blankets, 75 tons of bacon, 38,000 bushels of corn, and 92,000 uniforms and accoutrements were still in warehouses in Raleigh, awaiting distribution.

One of the greatest resources that the state contributed to the Confederate war effort was its manpower. With one-ninth of the population of the Confederacy, North Carolina supplied between one-sixth and one-seventh of the men in the Confederate army. During the war, it furnished seventy-two regiments, consisting of 110,000 troops, all of whom were volunteers save 19,000 conscripts, another 10,000 reserves in eight regiments, and 4,000 home guards. These came from a state with only 115,000 citizens eligible to vote in 1860. The state supplied over 51,000 stands of arms to its troops serving with Lee alone and spent over twenty-seven million dollars to field its men and material during the sectional conflict. North Carolina's total loss to battle and disease was 40,275, greater than that of any other Confederate state.

And yet, as rich as North Carolina might have been in men and raw materials, it, along with the other southern states, lacked heavy industry that in the long run would have such an important impact on the outcome of the war. In coastal North Carolina only two counties had ironworks: Chowan County had one and Craven County had two. Nowhere in the state did there exist facilities such as those found in Richmond, Norfolk, or New Orleans for the manufacture and repair of heavy ordnance and machinery. However, North Carolina did have a U.S. mint at Charlotte and a Federal arsenal at Fayetteville. Needless to say, the state immediately seized those facilities when the Civil War broke out.

Perhaps the state's greatest stride in improving transportation for the development of commerce on the coast was the establishment of railroads. In 1861 the South contained one-third of the nation's railways, and many of these lines used different gauges. North Carolina possessed 891 miles of rail, 651 miles of which was built after 1850. With state assistance, the Wilmington and Weldon and the Raleigh and Gaston Railroads were constructed and began operation in 1840. In 1849 the legislature chartered the North Carolina Railroad, which completed a line from Goldsboro through Raleigh to Charlotte in 1856. When the Wilmington and Weldon Railroad was finished it brought a surge in Wilmington's export trade, especially foreign. That railroad ran from the North Carolina port north to Petersburg, Virginia, and during the war it became a vital supply route for the Army of Northern Virginia. Until 1860 the chief commodity shipped on that railroad consisted of naval stores, but in that year wheat and cotton had overtaken naval stores, when the line shipped 31,000 bales of cotton and 84,000 bushels of wheat. The completion of that line also made it possible for Wilmington to leap ahead of New Bern, the other leading coastal port in foreign exports. On the eve of the sectional conflict, Wilmington, with a population of 9,552, and New Bern, with a population of 5,542, were the two largest towns in North Carolina. In 1858 workmen extended the Atlantic and North Carolina Railroad from Goldsboro to Morehead City via Kinston and New Bern. That helped to improve the shipping commerce of the ports of New Bern and Beaufort, but Wilmington remained the state's leading port. By the outbreak of the war, a large portion of the Wilmington, Charlotte, and Rutherfordton Railroad had also been finished, giving Wilmington further ties inland. The Wilmington and Manchester Railroad also gave Wilmington economic connections southward with Columbia and Charleston, South Carolina. On the coast, as throughout the state, the railroads had a significant impact on the economy of North Carolina. They cut in half old freight rates, and by encouraging the production of surplus crops for market, they increased the farmer's profits and decreased his costs. Railroads also led to the growth of the state's trade, revenue, and coastal towns such as Wilmington, New Bern, and Beaufort. Nevertheless, on the eve of the war, North Carolina remained largely undeveloped and economically deprived in comparison to its neighboring states to the north and south.

When the Civil War began, however, the coast of North Carolina held significant strategic value. Of supreme importance to the Confederacy and concern to the Union would be Wilmington, with its vital railway link to the Confederate army in Virginia and the dramatic component that kept that essential supply line operating—blockade-running!

On April 19, 1861, five days after the fall of Fort Sumter in Charleston Harbor, U.S. president Abraham Lincoln proclaimed a blockade of the seaports of six states that had seceded from the Union up to that point—South Carolina, Georgia, Alabama, Florida, Mississippi, and Texas. Eight days later he extended the blockade to include North Carolina and Virginia. At that point, the coastline of the new Confederate States of America extended 3,500 miles, from Cape Henry, Virginia, to the Gulf of Mexico, a distance longer than that from New York to Liverpool, England.

Yet despite this tremendous distance, few cities in the South had adequate port facilities and transportation to serve as lifelines to the outside world. The most promising were Norfolk, Beaufort/New Bern, Wilmington, Charleston, Savannah, Pensacola, Mobile, New Orleans, and Galveston, and to a far lesser extent, Key West and Saint Augustine. As the war wore on, the U.S. Navy tightened its grip on the Confederate coastline and one by one closed all blockade-running ports until in the last days of the conflict only North Carolina's Wilmington remained open. Before that coastal North Carolina port fell to Federal control in February 1865, it rendered—in large part because of the supplies and material procured through the blockade—a vital support without which the Confederacy probably would have crumbled much sooner than it did.

Throughout the Confederate coastal states, three hundred steamships tested the Federal blockade in thirteen hundred attempts, of which approximately 75 percent proved successful. On blockade-runners came 60 percent of the Confederacy's arms, one-third of its lead for bullets, three-quarters of the potassium nitrate for its gunpowder, nearly all its paper for cartridges, and the majority of its cloth and leather. Nearly one hundred blockade-runners, over one-half of which were eventually captured or sunk as the war progressed, regularly serviced Wilmington alone, bringing in no less than $65 million worth of irreplaceable goods. From the arrival of the *Theodora* on December 21, 1861, to the arrival of the *Wild Rover* on December 28, 1864, both from Nassau, Wilmington saw 303 arrivals of blockade-runners at its docks, carrying supplies for the Confederate war effort.

In addition to blockade-running, coastal North Carolina held other strategic importance during the Civil War. Federal possession of coastal North Carolina would place the Union army in the rear of the Confederate army in Virginia, as well as make it possible to threaten Norfolk from the sound region and force the Confederates to evacuate the port. From the coast the Federals could also raid the interior of North Carolina and strike at the Wilmington and Weldon Railroad, thereby cutting off large numbers of supplies meant for the Confederate regiments fighting in Virginia.

Therefore, the U.S. Army and Navy struck at the Tar Heel coast early in the Civil War and maintained a wartime presence there until the conflict ended in North Carolina in May 1865. During that period nine battles or significant skirmishes took place in the coastal region: Fort Hatteras (August 29, 1861), Roanoke Island (February 8, 1862), New Bern (March 14, 1862, March 13-14, 1863, and February 1-2, 1864), Fort Macon (April 26, 1862), Plymouth (April 17-20, 1864), and Fort Fisher at Wilmington (December 23-27, 1864, and January 13-15, 1865). Numerous Federal raids, such as that of Brig. Gen. Edward A. Wild and his African American troops into the northeastern counties in December of 1863, also brought the terror of war into the lives of coastal Tar Heels. The results of such conflagrations, the overall impact of Federal occupation and operations, and the response of coastal North Carolinians to the ravages of the Civil War are the subjects of the chapters that follow.

1 Reluctant to Leave the Union

North Carolina's decision to secede from the Union and join the Confederate States of America in May 1861 met with a reluctant response in the coastal region. In fact, during the tumultuous years leading up to the Civil War, the question of national loyalty and the political balance between the two political parties in North Carolina—the Democrats and the Whigs—had always been precarious in the counties along the coast.

Planters who owned large plantations and numbers of slaves in counties such as Craven usually joined with their neighbors in the western Coastal Plain and Piedmont in support of the Democratic Party, which generally resisted the efforts of the federal government to interfere in the rights of states to run their own affairs. The Democrats opposed such federal programs as aid for internal improvements, a protective tariff, and a national bank. At the root of the Democrats' opposition to federal intervention was the fear that the United States government would ultimately abolish slavery, an economic and social system upon which the plantation culture depended. A significant portion of the coast's residents, however, were working-class small farmers and fishermen, who owned few slaves and did not identify directly with the large plantation and slave economy. In large measure, they supported the Whig Party, which had been formed in the state in 1835 in opposition to the Democrats. The Whigs, who also found much support in the western part of the state as well as in the sound region, espoused federal support for internal improvements, a protective tariff, a national bank, public education, and humanitarian reform. Those inhabitants of the coast who supported the progressive programs of the Whig Party also adopted its principle of loyalty to the Union. The Whig Party dominated state politics from 1836 to 1850, when a wing of the Democratic Party endorsed some of the Whigs' progressive programs and regained control. But the prevailing sentiment in the state and the South primarily favored the slaveholding faction of the Democratic Party with its outspoken calls for states rights and extension of slavery into the territories acquired during the Mexican War. To guarantee those ideas, slaveholding Democrats began to consider secession from the Union.

Consequently, politics remained volatile in North Carolina as events propelled the state and nation toward civil war. In 1831 the rebellion of

Virginia slave Nat Turner and the publication of William Lloyd Garrison's abolitionist newspaper, the *Liberator*, increased the fear and resentment over the slavery issue throughout the South. The issue of slavery continued to dissolve the ties between North and South, as the Compromise of 1850, the Kansas-Nebraska Act of 1854, and the rise of the antislavery forces in the North intensified the dispute over the survival and perpetuation of the South's "peculiar institution." The fanatic abolitionist John Brown added to the fever of discord when he staged his unsuccessful raid on Harper's Ferry, Virginia, in 1859 in an effort to free slaves and lead them in an uprising against their masters. Fears that slavery might be extinguished had resulted in the dissolution of the Whig Party in 1854, and many members joined the newly formed Know-Nothing Party, but the Whigs revived in North Carolina four years later when conflict arose over the question of Democratic taxation policies that favored the wealthy planter class. In the gubernatorial election of 1860, a Whig candidate from coastal North Carolina, John Pool of Pasquotank County, ran against John Ellis of Rowan County. The coastal counties—with the exception of Chowan, Currituck, and Hyde—voted for Pool. But with the strong backing of the large plantation region, Ellis won the governorship.

The presidential election of 1860 brought to a climax the growing tension over slavery and sectionalism that strained the nation for much of the antebellum period. The Republican Party, which had been formed in 1856 and wanted to prohibit the spread of slavery into the territories, chose Abraham Lincoln as its candidate. So outraged at the antislavery Lincoln's candidacy were the southern states that they did not even allow the Republican candidate on their ballots. Because it could not reach a compromise on slavery in its platform, the Democratic Party split into two factions— northern and southern. The northern Democrats, who wanted the question of slavery in the territories determined by "popular sovereignty," nominated Stephen A. Douglas of Illinois as their candidate. The southern Democrats, who advocated the extension of slavery into the territories, selected John C. Breckinridge of Kentucky. But most of the counties of coastal North Carolina voted for yet a third, new party, which many of the old Whigs supported—the Constitutional Union Party formed in 1860. That party stood on a platform of strict allegiance to the Union and adherence to the U.S. Constitution. Its candidate for president was John Bell of Tennessee. With the exception of Currituck, Onslow, and New Hanover, which voted for the secessionist candidate Breckinridge, all the coastal

STATE OF NORTH CAROLINA.

A PROCLAMATION,

BY JOHN W. ELLIS,

GOVERNOR OF NORTH CAROLINA

WHEREAS: By Proclamation of Abraham Lincoln, President of the United States, followed by a requisition of Simon Cameron, Secretary of War, I am informed that the said Abraham Lincoln has made a call for 75,000 men to be employed for the invasion of the peaceful homes of the South, and for the violent subversion of the liberties of a free people, constituting a large part of the whole population of the late United States: And, whereas, this high-handed act of tyrannical outrage is not only in violation of all constitutional law, in utter disregard of every sentiment of humanity and Christian civilization, and conceived in a spirit of aggression unparalleled by any act of recorded history, but is a direct step towards the subjugation of the whole South, and the conversion of a free Republic, inherited from our fathers, into a military despotism, to be established by worse than foreign enemies on the ruins of our once glorious Constitution of Equal Rights.

Now, therefore, I, JOHN W. ELLIS, Governor of the State of North-Carolina, for these extraordinary causes, do hereby issue this, my Proclamation, notifying and requesting the Senators and Members of the House of Commons of the General Assembly of North-Carolina, to meet in Special Session at the Capitol, in the City of Raleigh, on Wednesday the first day of May next. And I furthermore exhort all good citizens throughout the State to be mindful that their first allegiance is due to the Sovereignty which protects their homes and dearest interests, as their first service is due for the sacred defence of their hearths, and of the soil which holds the graves of our glorious dead.

United action in defence of the sovereignty of North-Carolina, and of the rights of the South, becomes now the duty of all.

Given under my hand, and attested by the Great Seal of the State. Done at the City of Raleigh, the 17th day of April, A. D., 1861, and in the eighty-fifth year of our Independence,

JOHN. W. ELLIS.

By the Governor,
GRAHAM DAVES, *Private Secretary*.

North Carolina governor John W. Ellis issued this proclamation soon after the Confederate capture of Fort Sumter, South Carolina, and U.S. president Abraham Lincoln called for troops to suppress the rebellion. From the State Archives, Office of Archives and History, Raleigh.

counties voted for the Unionist Bell. The moderate Democrat Douglas received a smattering of votes in all the counties of the coast except Currituck.

The election of Lincoln enraged the South, and cries for secession echoed throughout the region. Not long after the election, the large slave-holding state of South Carolina seceded from the Union. Mississippi, Florida, Alabama, Georgia, Louisiana, and Texas had followed suit by February 1861. Those seven states subsequently formed the Confederate States of America.

But in North Carolina, without as large an interest in slavery, a majority of the citizens, including those on the coast, remained opposed to secession. Nevertheless, large slaveholding planters who favored secession continued to gain strength, and in January 1861 the General Assembly called for a convention to consider the question of withdrawing from the Union. North Carolinians, however, still wanting to remain part of the United States, voted against holding the convention, although by the narrow margin of 47,705 to 46,711. Those coastal counties in which over 50 percent of the voters supported the convention were Currituck, Craven, Onslow, New Hanover, and Brunswick.

Soon Confederate and United States officials met at a peace conference in Washington, D.C., in an effort to reconcile differences and avoid war. But that conference failed, and on April 12, 1861, Confederate artillery fired upon a Federal garrison at Fort Sumter in Charleston Harbor. In response, Lincoln called for troops from all the loyal states to help suppress the rebellion and restore the seceded states back into their proper relationship with the Federal government. Governor Ellis replied to the request: "You can get no troops from North Carolina." Ellis then ordered the seizure of Federal forts and other installations in the state. On the coast, North Carolina troops seized Forts Johnston and Caswell at Wilmington and Fort Macon at Beaufort Inlet. The outbreak of hostilities united most Unionists and secessionists in the state. The legislature called for a special convention to consider secession, which met in Raleigh on May 20, 1861. The convention passed an ordinance of secession and ratified the provisional constitution of the Confederate States of America. Thus the Old North State committed itself to the Confederacy and the ensuing civil war. It was not long before the reality of that war touched the coast of North Carolina.

2 The Federals Attack Hatteras

Shortly after its secession from the Union, North Carolina began efforts to defend its coast. The state created two departments of coastal defense. Brigadier Generals Walter Gwynn (a native of Virginia) and Theophilus Holmes supervised those departments. Gwynn commanded the northern department, which extended from Virginia to the New River in Onslow County. Holmes was in charge of the southern department, comprising the coast from the New River to South Carolina. Workmen started construction at Fort Fisher near the mouth of the Cape Fear River. As the war wore on, that fortification proved vital for the protection of the blockade-running port of Wilmington. The state also constructed forts at each of the unguarded inlets of the Outer Banks: Fort Oregon at Oregon Inlet, Fort Ocracoke (or Fort Morgan) inside Ocracoke Inlet, and Forts Hatteras and Clark at Hatteras Inlet. In May 1861 state troops had arrived at Cape Hatteras to protect the fifty-nine-year-old, ninety-foot-tall octagonal sandstone lighthouse situated there.

North Carolina native Gen. Theophilus Holmes helped supervise the preparation of the state's coastal defenses against Federal attack. Photograph from the State Archives.

Also to protect its coast, North Carolina acquired a small navy, which it quickly turned over to the Confederacy. It was commanded by Commodore Samuel Barron, who was in charge of the Confederate naval defenses of North Carolina and Virginia. That "mosquito fleet" consisted of four vessels: the *Winslow*, a side-wheel steamer; and the *Ellis*, the *Raleigh*, and the *Beaufort*. The last three were small, propeller-driven river boats and confined their operations to the sounds and rivers. The *Winslow*, however, steamed to Hatteras Inlet and for six weeks in the summer of 1861, that vessel, commanded by Capt. Thomas M. Crossan, reportedly captured sixteen ships traversing the Outer

In May 1861, North Carolina troops arrived at Cape Hatteras to protect the fifty-nine-year-old sandstone lighthouse (predecessor to the present lighthouse) located at that site. Champney drawing of the lighthouse from the Outer Banks History Center.

Banks. Thus the capacity to provide an outlet to raid Federal shipping gave Hatteras Inlet and its fortifications a primary significance. Furthermore, as David Stick, foremost historian of the Outer Banks, has noted, "Hatteras Inlet was at the time, the only inlet in the Outer Banks which could admit large ocean-going vessels." During the summer of 1861, over one hundred blockade-runners passed through the inlet.

The U.S. naval officer commanding the squadron blockading the Atlantic coast from Alexandria, Virginia, to Key West, Florida, was Flag Officer Silas Horton Stringham. His squadron, originally known as the Coast Blockading Squadron, soon was renamed the Atlantic Blockading Squadron. In September Stringham resigned, and the Blockade Strategy Board would divide the squadron into two divisions—north and south. The North Atlantic Blockading Squadron, commanded by Capt. Louis M. Goldsborough, held responsibility for the Federal blockade north of the North Carolina-South Carolina line. When he assumed command in September, Goldsborough found that he had only thirteen vessels to cover the waters of North Carolina and Virginia, excluding the Potomac River.

In the spring and summer of 1861, an acute shortage of ships to guard the North Carolina coast and prevent the raids of the *Winslow* and other vessels kept the U.S. Navy from effectively controlling Confederate activities along the Outer Banks. In May 1861 only two Union ships were on guard along the entire North Carolina coast. On July 11, 1861, workmen at Fort Oregon reported sporadic shelling by the USS *Roanoke*. Eleven days later, the USS *Albatross*, armed with two rifled cannon, engaged the CSS *Beaufort*, armed with one thirty-two-pound smoothbore, within sight of the unfinished parapets of Fort Oregon. The *Beaufort* was forced to retire. With these exceptions, Confederate defense preparation on the sounds and Outer Banks progressed without incident through the summer. What the few Union vessels that patrolled the area found was that the rough weather at Hatteras forced them to stay far out to sea. Volatile weather, for example, forced the U.S. screw steamer *Stars and Stripes* to use two anchors and her steam engine to hold a position off Hatteras on one occasion.

Thus virtually unmolested, work on Forts Hatteras and Clark soon reached completion. Fort Hatteras, the principal fort, stood near the inlet and commanded the channel. The octagonal fort, which occupied three-quarters of an acre, was constructed of sand with parapets rising to a height of ten feet. The smaller Fort Clark, a square redoubt made of reinforced sand, was located east of Hatteras and closer to the ocean. Completed in June, Fort Hatteras mounted twelve thirty-two-pound smoothbore guns, as well as a ten-inch Columbiad. Construction of Fort Clark concluded in July. That facility mounted six thirty-two pounders, two six-pound barbette guns, and could provide cross fire on the channel. By the time that Fort Hatteras was ready for occupancy, several companies of the Seventeenth Regiment North Carolina Troops (First Organization) and Company K, First Regiment North Carolina Artillery (Tenth Regiment North Carolina State Troops) had arrived as a garrison. On July 25, Maj. W. B. Thompson, the chief Confederate military engineer at Hatteras, reported that Fort Clark was fully operational, adding that Hatteras "is the key to Albemarle Sound, and it cannot be too strictly guarded." But despite Thompson's admonition, Confederate forces at Hatteras, Oregon, and Ocracoke Inlets totaled no more than 580 men by early August, with only 350 of them at Hatteras.

But even before work on the forts was completed, Union general Benjamin F. Butler, a former Massachusetts politician commanding at Fort Monroe, Virginia, notified the U.S. War Department that North Carolinians were building fortifications at Hatteras Inlet, which was a "depot for the rebel privateers." He suggested a small expedition to capture the forts. The War Department apparently disregarded Butler's suggestion, but the navy saw merit in his proposal and outlined a joint army-navy campaign against Hatteras, with Stringham in charge of the naval force and Butler commanding the army contingent. The plan called for the expedition to stop the Confederate privateering raids by the *Winslow* and others and to cut off the influx of supplies into North Carolina through Hatteras Inlet. According to their orders, Stringham and Butler were to capture the forts

In August 1861, U.S. general Benjamin F. Butler led an expedition to capture Forts Hatteras and Clark, which North Carolina had constructed at Hatteras Inlet. Photograph from the State Archives.

at Hatteras and then obstruct the channel with the so-called "stone fleet," schooners loaded with stone and towed to the inlet and sunk to block the passage of blockade-runners and other Confederate ships.

For the expedition, Butler had under his command elements of the Ninth and Twentieth Regiments New York Infantry and the Second Regiment United States Artillery, totaling 860 men, all of whom were stationed at that time near Fort Monroe. On August 25, 1861, Maj. Gen. John Wool, who had replaced Butler in command at Fort Monroe, authorized the troops to board the navy vessels waiting at nearby Hampton Roads. The following day, with ten days' rations and 140 rounds of ammunition per soldier, the fleet departed for Hatteras.

The commander of the Federal naval contingent for the attack on Forts Hatteras and Clark was Flag Officer Silas Horton Stringham. Photograph of engraving from the State Archives.

As it left Hampton Roads, the Federal squadron consisted of eight vessels: the steam frigates USS *Minnesota* (47 guns) and USS *Wabash* (46 guns); the gunboats USS *Monticello* (3 guns), USS *Pawnee* (9 guns), and USS *Fanny* (2 guns); the U.S. Revenue Cutter *Harriet Lane* (5 guns); and two transport ships, the *Adelaide* and the *George Peabody*, carrying men and equipment. As the expedition rounded Cape Henry, at the mouth of Chesapeake Bay, it was joined by the sloop USS *Cumberland* (24 guns) and the sidewheel steamer USS *Susquehanna* (15 guns). The ships then proceeded to the Outer Banks; only when the squadron was safely at sea were the soldiers, sailors, and junior grade officers told of their destination.

At 4:00 P.M. on August 27, 1861, the Union flotilla sighted the rebel forts at Cape Hatteras. As far as the Federals could discern, Fort Hatteras was the best defended of the two Confederate positions. It could be approached only over five hundred yards of flat terrain culminating in a narrow causeway that was open to canister and grapeshot from the fort's defenders. With dusk fast approaching, the ships remained off the cape, out of range of Confederate artillery and the treacherous shoals, and awaited the morning to attack.

The weather the next morning was typical of the cape in late summer;

strong winds created a heavy surf that thundered down upon the beaches, and the sky was dark and threatening. The original battle plan called for the ships to concentrate their fire on Fort Hatteras in order to cover the troops' landings. But that plan had to be changed when it was discovered that, due to shifting sandbars, ships drawing more than eighteen feet of water, which included the *Minnesota* and the *Wabash*, could safely approach no closer than one mile from Fort Hatteras. Butler therefore decided to land his troops further up the shore and concentrate the Union flotilla's fire on Fort Clark instead.

The *Adelaide* and the *George Peabody* had towed two hulks to the site to be used for landing troops in the attack. In mid-morning the troops boarded the hulks and drifted into the breakers by means of several sturdy cables that were attached to an anchor and passed around a windlass fixed onto the deck of each hulk. While the troop landings were under way, protected by the guns of the *Monticello* and the *Harriet Lane*, the other Federal ships, steaming in a circle to spoil the enemy's aim, engaged Fort Clark. The rebels vigorously returned the fire at first, but, finding that their shots were falling short and that they were running low on powder, they soon diminished their fire. Despite the volume of Federal bombardment, Fort Clark sustained relatively minor damage during the barrage.

By mid-afternoon, 318 Union soldiers had landed on the beach three miles from Fort Clark. This contingent was composed of men from the Ninth New York Regiment, commanded by a Captain Jardine; troops from the Twentieth New York Regiment, led by a Lieutenant Colonel Weiss; soldiers from the Second United States Artillery, under a Lieutenant Larned; crewmen of the Revenue Cutter Service, commanded by a Captain Nixon; and sailors and marines from the *Minnesota*. However, the surf became too heavy to land the troops still aboard the hulks, and there was no way for the men ashore to return to their ships, which had moved further out to sea to avoid grounding. In addition, one of the last hulks to land had been partially swamped, wetting powder and slightly damaging the carriage of a 12-pound howitzer. The other artillery piece already ashore, a 12-pound rifled gun, was undamaged.

Making the best of a poor situation, Lieutenant Colonel Weiss, the ranking Federal officer ashore, decided to reconnoiter with a detachment of twenty men down the beach toward Fort Clark. He returned in the early evening to report that it was being evacuated and its garrison retreating into Fort Hatteras. Unknown to the U.S. troops at this time, the Confeder-

The *Harriet Lane* became General Butler's flagship during the attack on Forts Hatteras and Clark. Photograph of engraving from the State Archives.

ates were not abandoning Fort Clark because of Union bombardment but because they had run out of powder.

The rebel defenders quickly spiked the cannons at the fort, lacking the means of transporting them, and retired south toward Fort Hatteras.

Captain Nixon then ordered his Revenue Cutter Service unit to proceed down the beach and occupy the now-empty fort. That was accomplished without opposition. A moment of consternation ensued when Federal ships, unaware of the evacuation of Fort Clark, commenced a long-range bombardment of the position now held by their own troops. Quickly, the men in the fort raised the "Stars and Stripes," and the firing ceased. With night fast approaching, the remaining landing party moved down the beach and joined the other troops in the fort. Pickets were set out around the fort, and a three-gun battery was established facing toward the Pamlico Sound to prevent any Confederate attempts to reinforce Fort Hatteras or assault Fort Clark from that direction.

Such an attack was exactly what the Confederates intended to do. The rebel commander of Fort Clark, Col. R. C. Bradford, once inside Fort Hatteras learned that its commander, Col. W. F. Martin, had already sent word to New Bern and Plymouth, North Carolina, that reinforcements were urgently needed. Martin told Bradford that those reinforcements, when they arrived, would be used, along with the companies of the Seventeenth Regiment and the First North Carolina Artillery already at Hatteras, to capture Fort Clark before the Federals could strengthen their position. Despite this plan, Martin's plea for reinforcements did not reach the authorities in New Bern until the Confederate situation at Hatteras was already lost.

At 8:00 A.M. on the morning of August 29, the Federal squadron moved

At Cape Hatteras, the Confederate forts of Clark and Hatteras fell quickly to the Union attack. This engraving depicts the shelling of Fort Hatteras on the second day of the attack. Copy from the State Archives.

in from its offshore position to recommence firing, this time at Fort Hatteras. The rebels returned the fire, striking the *Minnesota* once but causing little damage and no injuries. Before long, a white flag appeared above the ramparts of the fort. Commodore Stringham sent some officers ashore from the *Fanny* to ask the Confederate commander if he would surrender.

During the night, Commodore Samuel Barron arrived at Fort Hatteras aboard the *Winslow*. Both Colonels Bradford and Martin, being rather inexperienced with coastal fortifications, deferred to the judgment of that senior naval officer. Much to Barron's dismay, most of the fort's powder was either wet or of poor quality; in addition, the fuses on the Confederate shells were damaged or defective, and all of them were detonating short of their targets. The solid shot that could reach the Federal ships did little damage to them, while the Federals poured shot and shell down upon the rebels continuously. The reinforcements from New Bern had not arrived, and to finish matters, a Union shell had fallen down the fort's magazine

Troops from the Twentieth New York Regiment landing near Fort Hatteras.
Photograph of engraving from the State Archives.

ventilator and started a fire below, threatening the ammunition stored there. With no hope of success and little hope of relief, Barron advised that a white flag be raised in order to ask for terms of surrender.

Butler, who had left the *Harriet Lane*, his flagship, and joined Stringham aboard the *Minnesota*, received the Confederate request and replied that unconditional surrender was the only terms that would be accepted. Butler sent word that Fort Hatteras had less than one hour to surrender before Federal ships would again open fire. An anxious moment occurred when the *Harriet Lane*, waiting to receive a response, grounded on a sandbar directly under the guns of the fort. The Confederates, however, did not open fire on the stranded ship and instead decided to avoid further unnecessary bloodshed by surrendering. Before capitulating, though, Barron ordered that the *Winslow* be loaded with as many Confederate soldiers as possible and sent to New Bern to avoid capture. Once that was done, Barron and Martin boarded the *Fanny*, which took them out to the *Minnesota* to sign the documents of surrender. Soon afterward, the remaining Federal soldiers landed and occupied Fort Hatteras. The "Stars and Stripes" were raised over the works, accompanied by cheers and a thirteen-gun salute from the fleet.

In addition to seizing the two forts, the Federal expedition captured 715 prisoners, one thousand small arms, thirty cannons (some unmounted) and the 10-inch Columbiad, five small boats loaded with provisions, and five flags. That victory was won at almost no cost to the Federal army and navy, which suffered only one wounded soldier; the Confederates lost twelve killed and thirty-five wounded. Butler had a temporary wharf constructed to facilitate the transportation of the wounded, who were loaded on board the *Adelaide*, at which time the squadron returned to Fort Monroe

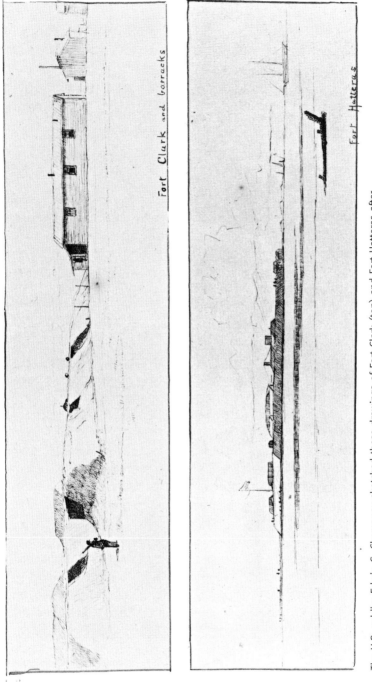

The U.S. soldier Edwin G. Champney sketched these drawings of Fort Clark (top) and Fort Hatteras after Federal troops captured those fortifications. Champney drawings from the Outer Banks History Center.

CHAPTER TWO

An artillery piece at Fort Clark. Champney drawing from the Outer Banks History Center.

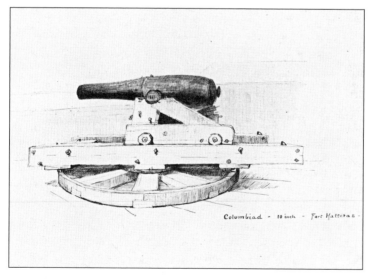

A 10-inch Columbiad at Fort Hatteras. Champney drawing from the Outer Banks History Center.

with the prisoners as well. Butler left Col. Rush Hawkins in command of the position until fresh troops could be sent. Hawkins's force then consisted of several companies of his own Ninth New York Zouaves, the Twentieth New York, and the vessels *Monticello*, *Pawnee*, and *Fanny*. As a result of losing Forts Hatteras and Clark, the Confederates were forced to form a new defense on Roanoke Island.

In Washington, D.C., the authorities were delighted with their success, which required such little effort. The specter of Cape Hatteras as a center for widespread privateering had been eliminated, and the Atlantic Blockading Squadron had an additional coaling station on the eastern seaboard. At first, General Butler—who subsequent to Hatteras commanded in New Orleans and the Army of the James in Virginia—believed that the climate and apparent lack of fresh water prevented establishing a large fortified Federal position and garrison at Cape Hatteras. But by the time he made his official report following the Federal success at Hatteras, he had come to realize the strategic importance that the cape and the inlet had for future Federal operations in North Carolina. In his report he declared that

> the importance of the [cape] cannot be overrated, when the channel is buoyed out any vessel may carry 15 feet of water over it with ease. Once inside, there is a safe harbor and anchorage in all weathers, from there, the whole coast of North Carolina, from Norfolk to Cape Lookout, is within our reach by light-draught vessels, which cannot possibly live at sea during the winter months. From it, offensive operations may be made upon the whole coast of North-Carolina, to Bogue inlet, extending many miles inland to Washington, New Berne, and Beaufort. In my judgement, it is station second in importance only to Fortress Monroe on this coast, [and] as a depot for coaling and supplies for the blockading squadron it is invaluable.

Although Butler has been regarded by historians as one of the Civil War's most incompetent political generals, his remarks about Hatteras were insightful and prophetic. For the U.S. War Department too would soon realize the possibilities that the control of Hatteras Inlet had opened for further "offensive operations . . . upon the whole coast of North-Carolina."

Meanwhile, since the capture of Forts Hatteras and Clark, the Federal garrison had been engaged in securing the area against any possible rebel attempts to recapture it. Colonel Hawkins ordered the forts repaired and enlarged. Fresh water was fairly abundant, but food was running low as the troops had only been issued ten-days' rations, when they had departed on the expedition. On September 10, six additional companies of the Ninth New York Regiment and sorely needed provisions arrived from Fort Monroe; the troops of the Ninth Regiment replaced some of the Twentieth New York Regiment who had been accused of vandalizing civilian property while at Hatteras and ordered back to Fort Monroe by General Wool.

The Federal garrison continued to fear attack. A few days before the reinforcements arrived, Comdr. J. P. Gillis of the *Monticello* reported while on a routine reconnaissance of Pamlico Sound that a rebel fort to the south of Hatteras at Ocracoke Island appeared to be deserted, and he strongly suggested taking it to prevent the rebels from using it in the future as a base of operations against Hatteras. Once the Federal reinforcements had arrived, Hawkins decided to act against the Confederate position at Ocracoke. On September 16, a detachment of men under Lt. J. G. Maxwell aboard the *Pawnee* left for Ocracoke. They found the fort deserted but containing four 7-inch guns and fourteen navy 32-pounders. Unable to occupy the fort permanently and lacking the means of transporting the guns back to Hatteras, Maxwell's men proceeded to break the trunnions off each cannon, rendering them useless to the rebels should they return later.

Despite the lack of evidence of any substantial rebel activity in the area since the Federals arrived, Colonel Hawkins was nevertheless concerned about a possible Confederate counterattack. He doubted that his current command, numbering 946 men, could resist a determined Confederate assault. Paradoxically in light of those fears, Hawkins, on September 19, ordered four companies of the Ninth New York to proceed four miles from Fort Clark and establish a base later known as Camp Wool, with pickets placed two miles beyond that, in order to give the Federals control of the southern-most six miles of Hatteras Island. Hawkins defended the splitting of his already small command by saying that Camp Wool could warn Forts Clark and Hatteras should the Confederates attempt to surprise the Federal position from the north.

Hawkins also made an effort to gather as much intelligence on enemy activities as possible from the local inhabitants, but most of what he received was greatly exaggerated or wholly inaccurate. For example, he received reports that Fort Macon, near Beaufort to the south, had been reinforced with railroad iron, stocked with new guns of all sizes, and occupied by 4,500 elite troops. New Bern was said to have new guns, two full-

Following the Union success at Hatteras Inlet, the Twentieth Indiana Regiment marched north to establish a base at Chicamacomico. When the U.S. steamer *Fanny* attempted to supply the regiment at that base, she was captured by Confederate vessels. Photograph of engraving of the *Fanny* from the State Archives.

strength regiments, three squadrons of cavalry, and a section of light artillery. Hawkins became especially disturbed on September 21, when he spoke to the runaway slaves of one Samuel Jarvis, who lived on Roanoke Island. They told him that the rebels currently had over 8,000 infantry on the island preparing to recapture Hatteras, destroy the lighthouse, and hang all of the local Union sympathizers. Of course, those reports were false, as later events would tell, but they nevertheless gave the Federal garrison at Hatteras some sleepless nights.

Then again Hawkins acted paradoxically. After receiving reinforcements of three hundred men and supplies on September 29, he sent those men, of the Twentieth Regiment Indiana Infantry, to establish a base forty miles north of Cape Hatteras at Chicamacomico, ostensibly to protect any Union sympathizers among the locals and warn of any impending attack. Not only did that further divide his command, but it also presented new problems in communications and supply. Trouble quickly occurred. On October 1, the *Fanny* steamed north in the sounds to bring supplies to the newly established base at Chicamacomico. While the vessel had a master and mate aboard, it was largely manned by soldiers of the Twentieth Indiana, who were not seasoned seamen. Col. D. M. Brown of the Twentieth

Indiana was slow in ordering his men to unload the supplies, and consequently the *Fanny* could not begin the return trip to Hatteras Inlet until late in the afternoon. At the same time, 150 Confederates of the Third Regiment Georgia Volunteer Infantry from Roanoke Island, aboard the steamers CSS *Junaluska*, CSS *Raleigh*, and CSS *Curlew*, were headed for Chicamacomico to investigate the rumors of a Federal base there. Unexpectedly, those steamers intercepted the *Fanny* as it was leaving, ran it aground, and after a brief struggle, captured the ship intact.

The capture raised Confederate morale. A Confederate officer at Roanoke Island later wrote: "the victory was important in more respects than one. It was our first naval success in North Carolina and the first capture made by our arms of an armed war vessel of the enemy, and dispelled the gloom of recent disasters. The property captured [two rifled guns and a large number of army stores, as well as the ship itself] was considerable, much needed, and highly esteemed."

After Hawkins learned of the loss of the *Fanny*, he realized the imminent danger to his split command and ordered his troops at Chicamacomico to return to Hatteras Inlet at once. By the time his order reached the Twentieth Indiana, though, those troops were already under attack. The Confederates on Roanoke Island, heartened by the capture of the *Fanny*, decided to attack the forces at Chicamacomico before they could be reinforced or withdrawn. Commodore William F. Lynch—a Virginian and former U.S. Navy captain who had taken over command of North Carolina's Confederate naval forces when Commodore Barron had been captured and held prisoner by the Federals following the fall of the forts at Hatteras Inlet in August—gathered together as many of his steamers as possible to transport the assault troops from Roanoke Island to Chicamacomico. Elements of the Third Georgia Infantry and Eighth Regiment North Carolina State Troops (Infantry), under the command of Col. A. R. Wright of the Third Georgia, were selected for the attack. A civilian visitor to Roanoke Island on October 3 found the officers and men "all very busy in making preparations and embarking troops." He continued:

> I remained with them until just before they left. The scene was very animated. The evening was calm and the sound smooth as glass. Steamers and barges crowded with troops were anchored off the shore. Cheers of welcome arose from the troops on board as new companies marched down to embark. . . . from one steamer the lively notes of "Dixie" filled the air; from another the notes of

the violin floated on the air, and from others the solemn service of praise and prayer to God went up from the mingled voices.

The Confederates attacked on the morning of October 4, 1861. Their battle plan called for the Third Georgia to attack from the north and the Eighth North Carolina to land south of Chicamacomico and catch the Federals in a trap. Unfortunately for the Georgians, the barges carrying the North Carolina troops grounded, and the Twentieth Indiana and some loyal inhabitants were able to withdraw hastily, starting what came to be known as the "Chicamacomico Races." The Confederates pursued the fleeing Federals for many miles, but as night fell they stopped and bivouacked. Hawkins, learning that evening what had happened to the Indiana regiment, ordered the *Monticello* and elements of the Ninth New York to counterattack the next morning. Lying three-quarters of a mile offshore, the *Monticello* shelled the Confederate camp as the New York regiment proceeded to chase the rebels back to Chicamacomico. The end

Fearing Confederate attack, the Twentieth Indiana fled from Chicamacomico back to Hatteras Inlet. The regiment bivouacked at the base of the Cape Hatteras Lighthouse on the night of October 4, 1861. Photograph of engraving from the State Archives.

CHAPTER TWO

Union troops remained on Hatteras Island throughout the war. Some of them occupied the house of the lighthouse keeper. Champney drawings from the Outer Banks History Center.

result of the "races" was negligible; losses on both sides were slight, with the Confederates returning to Roanoke Island and the Federals withdrawing to Camp Wool. Both sides claimed victory.

But Hawkins's superiors were not pleased with his performance. By unnecessarily dividing his command, Hawkins had endangered Forts Clark and Hatteras, they maintained. The Twentieth Indiana, in its haste to escape the enemy, had left all of its supplies at Chicamacomico and was then in a state of great want of blankets and clothing at Camp Wool. Hawkins tried weakly to defend his actions, saying that by not sending him more reinforcements, the Federal government was guilty of "criminal neglect." He added, "generals are made of such queer stuff nowadays that I should not esteem it any very great honor to be made one." That was all General Wool could bear. He recalled Hawkins to Fort Monroe and replaced him at Hatteras with Brig. Gen. Joseph K. F. Mansfield.

In retrospect, it is perhaps unfortunate for the Union war effort that the U.S. War Department did not make a more determined effort to penetrate inland in North Carolina immediately following the early Federal success on Hatteras Island in 1861. The Federals' perception of Confederate strength was exaggerated, and with additional light-draft vessels and more troops, the U.S. Army and Navy might have safely expanded its sphere of influence on the mainland. Most Confederate defensive works in the area were still unfinished and its defenders unprepared for invasion. But although the U.S. War Department did not immediately follow up on its victory at Hatteras Inlet, not many months would elapse before the Federals struck again at the coast of the Tar Heel State—this time with a greater force and sense of mission.

3 The Burnside Expedition Captures Roanoke Island

The North Atlantic Blockading Squadron was stretched so thin in the autumn of 1861 that President Lincoln at first agreed with those Federal officers who held that further offensive operations against the coast of North Carolina were inadvisable because such operations required a greater U.S. naval presence than that existing under the current situation. Nevertheless, the Union army soon began making plans for a second attack on the Tar Heel coast. Exactly who conceived the original plan for the "first major amphibious assault in United States history" is not certain. Both Maj. Gen. George B. McClellan and Brig. Gen. Ambrose E. Burnside would claim to have been the first to think of the idea. McClellan, a West Point graduate and prewar army officer and railroad executive, commanded the Army of the Potomac and in November would also replace Gen. Winfield Scott as commander in chief of the Federal armies, serving in that capacity until July 1862. Burnside—a West Point man, prewar army officer and manufacturer, and a friend and subordinate of McClellan—would eventually command the new expedition.

Not long after he assumed command of the Army of the Potomac in the summer of 1861, McClellan had taken a keen interest in the opportunities afforded by coastal operations along the Atlantic seaboard—including North Carolina. On September 4, he had dinner with Comdr. Charles H. Davis, chairman of the Blockade Strategy Board, who had helped plan and organize the North Atlantic Blockading Squadron and the attack on Hatteras Inlet. As word of the capture of Fort Hatteras had just reached Washington, the dinner conversation naturally turned to developments in North Carolina. Apparently McClellan impressed Davis with his enthusiasm for further coastal operations there. U.S. commanding general Winfield Scott, however, did not share McClellan's enthusiasm. As author of the strategic "Anaconda Plan" in which the blockade played such an important role in "squeezing" the Confederacy into submission, Scott saw the coast of North Carolina as being vital only as a coaling station for the blockading squadron. He was supported in his view by Brig. Gen. Joseph K. F. Mansfield, with whom General Wool had replaced Colonel Hawkins at Hatteras. In October Mansfield reported directly to Scott that Cape Hatteras was wholly inadequate as a base of operations against the mainland.

But McClellan took little notice of such objections and continued to make plans for further invasion of the Carolina coast. On September 12, he instructed Burnside to begin raising a force of two brigades from New England to form the core of a coastal division for possible operations on the coast of Virginia and North Carolina. Burnside later recalled that his orders were

> to organize in the eastern states regiments near the sea coast, composed as much as possible of men who know more or less about steamers sailing vessels, surf boats, &c., and to arm and equip a sufficient number of vessels of light draught to carry this division of men [approximately 10,000] so that they could be moved quickly from one point on the coast to another. The object in arming these vessel with heavy guns was to enable them to overcome any slight opposition that they might meet with on the rivers or coast, without the necessity of waiting for assistance from the navy which might not be at hand. All of those vessels were to be well supplied with surfboats, launches, and other means of landing troops. The vessels were to be of the lightest draught possible, in order to navigate all the bays, harbors, and rivers of the waters of the Chesapeake Bay and of North Carolina.

As the autumn wore on, Federal authorities in Washington began to warm to McClellan's ideas for coastal operations. Receptivity to such plans increased with the news that the stone fleet at Hatteras Inlet was not producing the anticipated results of deterring Confederate blockade- runners. On November 1, Scott resigned, and McClellan, while still commanding the Army of the Potomac, became commanding general of the Union armies.

Meanwhile, General Wool at Fort Monroe became increasingly concerned that the garrison at Cape Hatteras should either be reinforced or withdrawn. On November 5, he dispatched to Washington Colonel Hawkins, who had returned to Fort Monroe when Wool recalled him from Hatteras. Hawkins's instructions were to persuade the president of the necessity of reinforcing and strengthening Fort Hatteras and rotating troops from Fort Monroe, or else withdrawing the Hatteras garrison altogether. Hawkins realized the importance of holding Cape Hatteras and

Gen. Ambrose E. Burnside commanded the U.S. Army expedition to capture Roanoke Island in January 1862. Engraving from *Dictionary of American Portraits* (New York: Dover Publications, 1967), 90.

took it upon himself to urge reinforcement over withdrawal. For weeks, Hawkins had been urging his superiors to reinforce the cape and allow for offensive action. In one of his numerous letters to Secretary of War Simon Cameron, he claimed that "7,000 men judiciously placed upon the soil of North Carolina would draw 20,000 Confederate troops from the state of Virginia" to combat the Federal invasion to their rear. But so far his suggestion had been ignored. Once in Washington, he was summoned to appear at a meeting of the president and the cabinet. McClellan was at the meeting in place of the secretary of war.

Hawkins presented his viewpoint, and McClellan spoke in support of the idea. Secretary of the Navy Gideon Welles also leaned toward an invasion of coastal North Carolina. Realizing that the "stone fleet" was not proving to be a successful obstacle to Confederate shipping, he felt that invasion of mainland North Carolina might actually release ships for duty elsewhere, especially if Federal troops seized specific ports that were the destinations of blockade-runners. Lincoln and his cabinet became persuaded of the benefits of an invasion of the Carolina coast: the threat to the enemy's rear in Virginia and to Norfolk and the Chesapeake Bay area; the ability to strike at the Wilmington and Weldon Railroad and cut off supplies to the Confederate army in Virginia; as well as to hamper blockade-running; and even possibly driving inland and eventually connecting with Federal regiments pushing into North Carolina from Tennessee, thus splitting the Confederacy. Perhaps one last important factor helped to sway Lincoln on the plan. Throughout his presidency, Lincoln hoped to draw upon the support of Unionists in the Confederate states to help him establish governments within those states that would swear loyalty to the Federal government and enable him to bring those states back into the Union under his tentative plans for wartime reconstruction. Because coastal North Carolina had a large number of Unionists, Lincoln reasoned, it might prove to be the best locale for launching such a plan for the reconstruction and restoration of North Carolina to the Union. On September 7, Hawkins had reported to General Wool about the extent of Union sentiment in the coastal counties of the Tar Heel State:

> I have been informed by some [inhabitants] that secret union meetings have been held in several of the counties bordering on Pamlico Sound, and that they would openly avow themselves true to the United States government if they were sure that they would be protected against the violence of the secessionists. It is also thought that a union convention would be called at once, and that these counties would vote themselves back into the Union and take up arms to defend themselves if necessary. . . . I have no doubt that one-third of the state of North Carolina would be back in the Union within two weeks.

Such was the lure of a regionally strong Unionist population, that Lincoln continued to hope and plan for a loyal Unionist government in coastal North Carolina throughout a large part of the war. (See Chapter 6.)

Following the cabinet meeting of November 1861, the War and Navy Departments began making plans for the invasion of coastal North Carolina. General Burnside would command the army component of the invasion. Commodore Goldsborough would command the support and transport vessels of the North Atlantic Blockading Squadron. The expedition would be hampered by the fact that both the army and navy gathered ships for the operation and retained control over their own vessels. Goldsborough referred to the entire floating contingent as his "paste-board fleet." The overall plan for operation called for Burnside's officers to assemble the troops aboard transport ships at Annapolis, Maryland, and along with a

Capt. Louis M. Goldsborough, flag officer of the North Atlantic Blockading Squadron, commanded the naval component of the Roanoke Island campaign. Engraving from *Dictionary of American Portraits*, 244.

CHAPTER THREE

number of army gunboats sail to Hampton Roads, near Fort Monroe, Virginia, where they would be joined by a flotilla from Goldsborough's naval squadron.

The initial objective of the Burnside expedition—as the coastal North Carolina operation came to be known—was Roanoke Island. The capture of that island would give the Federals a base from which to operate on the North Carolina sounds and possibly to recapture Norfolk. From Roanoke Island they could strike other sites along the inland waters of the state, and the navy could anchor its shallow-draft vessels in the sounds. Burnside's orders called for him to launch operations from the island to capture the important objectives of New Bern, Beaufort, Fort Macon, and the Albemarle and Chesapeake Canal. Then from his base on the coastal mainland, he could strike into the interior of the Tar Heel State. General McClellan's orders of January 7 read:

> The commodore and yourself having completed your arrangements in regard to Roanoke Island and the waters north of it, you will please at once make a descent on New Berne, having gained possession of which and the railroad passing through it, you will at once throw a sufficient force upon Beaufort and take the steps necessary to reduce Fort Macon and open that port. When you seize New Berne you will endeavor to seize the railroad as far west as Goldsborough, should circumstances favor such a movement. The temper of the people, the rebel force at hand, etc., will go far towards determining the question as to how far west the railroad can be safely occupied and held. Should circumstances render it advisable to seize and hold Raleigh, the main north and south line or railroad passing through Goldsborough should be so effectually destroyed for considerable distances north and south of that point as to render it impossible for the rebels to use it to your disadvantage. A great point would be gained, in any event, by the effectual destruction of the Wilmington and Weldon Railroad. I would advise great caution in moving so far into the interior as upon Raleigh. Having accomplished the objects mentioned, the next point interest would probably be Wilmington, the reduction of which may require that additional means shall be afforded you.

From the onset of the war, the Federal government had included the state of North Carolina in the army's Department of the East. That department, covering several of the southeastern coastal states, was too large to be conveniently managed, and it was soon deactivated. On August 17, 1861, General Wool at Fort Monroe assumed command of the newly created Department of Virginia, leaving the Department of the East without a commander. For the remainder of 1861, North Carolina, though still officially included in the inactive Department of the East, was considered an appendage of Wool's Department of Virginia, as the Union troops at Hatteras had come from his command. Toward the end of 1861, the territory previously covered by the Department of the East was divided into separate commands, and in preparation for the upcoming Roanoke Island campaign, the U.S. government removed North Carolina from Wool's department. On January 7, 1862, the newly created Department of North Carolina was established under General Burnside.

Two days before, on January 5, the harbor at Annapolis, Maryland, had been filled with activity. In preparation for his expedition, Burnside had carefully selected the regiments from the states of New York, New Jersey, Connecticut, Rhode Island, and Massachusetts, which soon assembled on transports bound for Fort Monroe. That coastal division consisted of three brigades, commanded by Brigadier Generals Jesse Reno, John G. Foster, and John Parke. Federal troops mustered on and around the grounds of the U.S. Naval Academy. General Foster's First Brigade (the Twenty-third, Twenty-fourth, Twenty-fifth, and Twenty-seventh Massachusetts, and the Tenth Connecticut infantry regiments) was to embark on its transport ships at the upper wharf of the Naval Academy. General Reno's Second Brigade (the Twenty-first Massachusetts, Sixth New Hampshire, Ninth New Jersey, Fifty-first New York, and Fifty-first Pennsylvania infantry regiments, plus elements of the First Regiment Rhode Island Light Artillery, Ninety-ninth New York, and First New York Marine Artillery) was assigned to the lower wharf. General Parke ordered the commanders of his Third Brigade (the Fourth Rhode Island, Fifth Rhode Island, Eighth Connecticut, Eleventh Connecticut, Fifty-third New York, and Eighty-ninth New York infantry regiments) to load at the nearby wharf serving the Naval Academy hospital. Union commanders envisioned that arrangement of embarkation sites as a way to speed the unwieldy process of loading and transporting such a large number of men, though even with the best of circumstances the process was still expected to take a full forty-eight hours.

To transport the three brigades—numbering over 15,000 men, along with their horses, supplies, and armaments—the army had present at

Annapolis twelve steamers: *City of New York, Cossack, Eastern Queen, Eastern State, George Peabody, Guide, Louisiana, New York, Pocahontas, Union, Northerner,* and *New Brunswick.* There were thirty-two army sailing vessels on hand: *Kitty Simpson, Martha Greenwood, Dragoon, Guerrilla, John Trucks, Ann Thompson, Aracan, Voltigueur, Emma, Edward Slade, Recruit, Highlander, Griswold, Glenwood, Farrington, Elizabeth Segur, Colonel Satterly, Scout, Seabird, Mary Banks, Brookman, Skirmisher, H. E. Pierce, James Brady, Maria Pike, N. S. Rue, Plandon, Roche, Sara Smith, Sara Mills, T. P. Larned,* and *William Crocker.* Nine armed, propeller-driven gunboats escorted the squadron: *Chasseur, Hussar, Lancer, Picket, Pioneer, Ranger, Sentinel, Vidette,* and *Zouave.* Five army floating batteries also accompanied the fleet: *Bombshell, Grapeshot, Grenade, Rocket,* and *Shrapnel.* The gunboats and floating batteries had a total of forty-seven guns.

Conditions aboard the army vessels were cramped and uncomfortable. The steamer *New York*, for example, had bunks stacked four atop one another, with only twenty inches in between, and were less than two feet wide. Mattresses were stuffed with either straw or dried seaweed, and there was no more than thirty inches in between bunks from side to side. The humidity and olfactory sensations were far from pleasant. Moreover, Burnside had assembled his armada from maritime odds and ends. The ships were converted coal barges, tugboats, passenger steamers, ferries, and propeller-driven vessels of all kinds. According to the general, they "had been strengthened from deck to keelson by heavy oak planks, and water-tight compartments had been built into them; they were so arranged that parapets of sand-bags or bales of hay could be built upon their decks, and each one carried from four to six guns. Sailing vessels, formerly belonging to the coasting trade, had been fitted up in the same manner." Some of the fleet were veterans of the Hatteras expedition. But the general impression was that a large number of the vessels were unseaworthy.

So prevalent was that opinion among officers and men, that when Burnside and Goldsborough joined the expedition at Fort Monroe, Burnside transferred his flag from the *George Peabody* to the small propeller-driven tug *Picket* as a show of confidence. With last minute preparations completed, the huge convoy left Hampton Roads for Hatteras on January 11, 1862.

As the fleet left the Roads, a number of naval warships joined the army ships for the trip south: USS *Henry Brinker,* USS *Delaware,* USS *Philadelphia,* USS *Hunchback,* USS *Morris,* USS *Southfield,* USS *Commodore Barney,* USS

Commodore Perry, USS *Ceres*, USS *Granite*, USS *Hetzel*, USS *William Putnam*, and USS *Howard*, all under the tactical command of Comdr. Stephen C. Rowan. In addition, Goldsborough had ordered the USS *Louisiana*, USS *Lockwood*, USS *Seymour*, USS *Shawseen*, and USS *Whitehall* to Hatteras Inlet to join the USS *Stars and Stripes*, USS *Underwriter*, and USS *Valley City* already on station there. According to plan, once the naval armada reached Hatteras there would be twenty-one naval warships of varying sizes present for duty, carrying a total of sixty-two guns, including fifteen ten-inch pieces. Many of those ships were chosen because of their relatively shallow draft, making them suitable for operations in the sounds. Early in January, Goldsborough had written to Burnside that "the sooner [we arrive at Hatteras] the better [in light of] all the vessels you have which require choice weather in order to arrive safely."

Goldsborough was justified in his warning against bad weather, for no sooner had the Federal fleet reached Cape Hatteras on the evening of January 13 than a terrible winter storm struck. Ships were tossed and battered mercilessly. Everything that was not lashed to the decks was washed overboard. So too were two officers of the Ninth New Jersey Infantry Regiment. For almost two weeks the fleet was lashed by one storm after another. The seas ran high, and the fog was dense. Those vessels near the bar at the inlet particularly suffered from the ferocious waves and wind. The floating battery *Grapeshot* and the gunboats *Zouave* and *Louisiana* were lost along with the *Pocahontas*, which was transporting one hundred horses. The *City of New York* grounded on the beach and was beaten to pieces in

When the Burnside expedition arrived off Cape Hatteras in January 1862, a tremendous storm struck. One of the Union ships that wrecked during the storm was the steamer *Pocahontas*. Engraving from the North Carolina Collection, Wilson Library, University of North Carolina at Chapel Hill.

　　　　　　　　　　　CHAPTER THREE

a matter of minutes. Burnside feared that the flagship *Picket* would be crushed by a larger vessel in the gale, so Goldsborough ordered the fleet to scatter until the storm passed. Thus separated from the ships carrying food and water, troops on a number of ships endured an acute shortage of rations and water for days. One soldier of the Twenty-fifth Massachusetts Regiment on board the *New York* described one of the storms:

> As far as the eye can see, the water is rolling, foaming and dashing over the shoals, throwing it's [sic] white spray far into the air as though the sea and sky meet. This is no time for man to war against man. The forces of Heaven are loose and in all their fury, the winds howls, the sea rages, the eternal is here in all his majesty. As one looks out on the grand yet terrible scene, he can but exclaim, "Great and marvelous are thy works, Lord, God Almighty!"

Finally on January 26 the weather cleared. But the fleet still faced another obstacle imposed by nature. Most of the vessels had little trouble in getting over the bar at Hatteras Inlet, but crossing the shallow swash into Pamlico

Once the bad weather cleared, the Union fleet still had to cross the shallow swash into Pamlico Sound. This engraving from the *Illustrated London News* shows several U.S. vessels crossing the shoals near Cape Hatteras. Copy from the State Archives.

Sound proved to be much more difficult. In order to pass over the swash, the fleet had to deepen the channel. Someone among the invading force developed a plan that was successfully implemented: "large vessels were sent ahead, under full steam, on the bar when the tide was running out, and then the anchors were carried out by boats in advance, so as to hold the vessels in position. As the tide ran out, the swift current would wash the sand from under them to float, after which they were driven farther on by steam and anchored again, when the sand would again wash out under them. The process was continued for days, until a broad channel . . . was formed." On February 4, the last ships of Burnside's expedition crossed the swash, and the following day those eighty vessels made for Roanoke Island.

In the meantime the Confederate War Department had made only meager efforts to defend the island. Since the fall of Cape Hatteras in August 1861, Gov. Henry T. Clark and other military officers of North Carolina became convinced that there would soon be a battle for control of coastal North Carolina. They generally concurred that the site of such an engagement would be Roanoke Island. But control of the defenses for the coast had passed to the Confederate government in Richmond, and all North Carolinians could do was press for troops and arms from the War Department. President Davis considered it "highly inexpedient" to withdraw troops from Virginia to defend the Tar Heel coast, and he informed Governor Clark that only new recruits and militia were available. Except for a few guns supplied by Secretary of the Navy Stephen R. Mallory, the plea for arms brought only promises.

But the War Department did dispatch Confederate officers to take charge of defenses in North Carolina. Brig. Gen. Richard C. Gatlin, a native of North Carolina and former adjutant general of the state, had been given command of the Department of North Carolina with headquarters at Goldsboro on August 16, 1861. Responsible for the state's coastal defenses, he had made repeated requests for gunboats, artillery, men, arms, and equipment but saw his pleas largely ignored and Cape Hatteras easily fall to Union attack. Brig. Gen. D. H. Hill, a South Carolina native but popular in North Carolina, who had been commanding troops in Virginia, had received command of the defense of Albemarle and Pamlico Sounds. After inspecting the troops and fortifications at Roanoke Island, Hill made the following report to the War Department:

Roanoke Island is the key of one-third of North Carolina, and whose occupancy by the enemy would enable him to reach the great railroad from Richmond to New Orleans. Four additional regiments are absolutely indispensable to the protection of this island. The batteries also need four rifled cannon of heavy caliber. I would most earnestly call the attention of the honorable Secretary of War to the importance of Roanoke Island. Its fall would be fully as fatal as that of Manassas. The enemy has now 8,000 men at Hatteras, and Roanoke Island will undoubtedly be attacked.

Hill also implored Gatlin to send reinforcements to Roanoke Island. Brig. Gen. Joseph R. Anderson of Virginia had taken charge at Wilmington on September 7, and he too beseeched Gatlin for troops.

Although Gatlin was sympathetic to Hill's request for reinforcements, he was unable to oblige him. Nevertheless, Hill ordered a line of defenses thrown up on the island, which included a direct line of earthworks to be constructed across the island and a relocation of a fort on the lower part of the island. Before these measures were carried out, however, Hill was transferred back to Virginia. The War Department then divided his former North Carolina command into two parts. The first, commanded by Brig. Gen. Henry A. Wise, former governor of Virginia, included the district extending from Norfolk to Roanoke Island. The second, commanded by Brig. Gen. L. O'B. Branch of North Carolina, consisted of the region around New Bern. Wise's area of command, including Roanoke Island, was then separated from the Department of North Carolina and placed in the Department of Norfolk commanded by Maj. Gen. Benjamin Huger.

While Burnside's fleet was stranded off Cape Hatteras by bad weather during much of January 1862, Wise hurried to Richmond to appeal to the president and the secretary of war for additional soldiers, but his request was denied again. When the Federals finally arrived off Roanoke Island, they found the fortifications and the troops manning them woefully inadequate.

Three turfed sand forts—Huger, Blanchard, and Bartow—mounting in total twenty-five guns, stood on the west side of the island. (Only the southernmost, Bartow, would be actively engaged in the upcoming battle, the other two being out of range.) On the east side of the island, the Confederate defenders had erected a two-gun emplacement at Ballast Point. In the middle of the island, an eighty-foot redoubt—a three-gun emplacement flanked by breastworks and a swamp—commanded the only road running north and south. Across Croatan Sound on the mainland was Fort Forrest, which had been constructed from two old barges pushed next to the shore. That fort mounted seven guns.

Initially to man those fortifications and defend the island, Wise had 1,473 soldiers. Those included 475 men of the Thirty-first Regiment North Carolina Troops, commanded by Col. John V. Jordan; 568 men of the Eighth Regiment North Carolina State Troops, commanded by Col. Henry M. Shaw; and 450 troops from the Forty-ninth and Fifty-ninth Regiments Virginia Volunteers under the command of Lt. Col. Frank P. Anderson. Earlier Col. A. R. Wright's Third Georgia Regiment had been withdrawn from the island. "Bad feeling" had developed between the North Carolina and Georgia troops, and Wright himself was disparaging of the Tar Heels. "The North Carolina companies here are completely disorganized and demoralized [and] I can hope for nothing from them," he declared.

A double line of sixteen sunken vessels obstructed Croatan Sound, and a system of pilings was still being hurriedly placed there as obstacles when Burnside arrived on the scene. Behind the sunken vessels and pilings floated Commodore Lynch's "Mosquito Fleet." The "Mosquito Fleet" included the gunboats Seabird, Appomattox, Curlew, Ellis, Beaufort, Raleigh, Forrest, the captured gunboat Fanny, and the schooner Black Warrior. Each ship carried a 32-pound gun, and its crew was largely foreigners who had been aboard vessels captured by the Confederate privateer Winslow. Other vessels in Lynch's fleet included the Winslow, Junaluska, Cotton Plant, Manassas, Sandfly, and Mosquito. With this motley collection of armed barges and tugboats, Lynch hoped to stop the Federal expedition. Luckily for the Confederate fleet, though Goldsborough's squadron boasted over sixty large guns, not all of these could be navigated into the shallow waters of the sounds.

While still off Hatteras, on February 3, Burnside issued general order number five, saying that the Federals had come to coastal North Carolina to support the United States Constitution and put down the lawless rebellion but that private property of law-abiding citizens would be respected. "In the march of the army, all unnecessary injury to houses, barns, fences, and other property will be carefully avoided, and in all cases the laws of civilized warfare will be strictly observed," the general proclaimed.

The Federal squadron left Hatteras on February 5 and traveled due north in Pamlico Sound, arriving at Stumpy Point, six miles from Roanoke Island at 5:30 P.M. The column of U.S. ships was eight miles in length. There they weighed anchor for the evening. Soldiers on board passed time by playing chess and checkers, cards, gambling (though technically forbidden), reading, writing, as well as grumbling and complaining. William Derby, a private of the Twenty-seventh Massachusetts Regiment, recorded his impression of the appearance of coastal North Carolina bordering the sounds:

> the marshes are fathomless swamps, where the vegetable mold has accumulated for ages, until sufficient consistency has formed to crowd the bilious waters into meandering streams and intersecting and dividing pools of stagnant water. Into the slimy depths of mire, huge cone shaped roots from the cypress plunge for sustenance and support, while monster trees rise, with distended paunch like trunks, towering aloft as if attempting to escape from their repulsive surroundings. Huge vines embrace their trunks like serpents, crossing from tree to tree, and mingling in interminable snarls, while the sweet briar, which forms the undergrowth, forbids admission to, or exit from, these confines. The river banks are low, disappearing almost imperceptibly at the waterline. Where ever the shore assumes solidity, scattering fishermen's homes cling close to [the water], the scant clearing around them showing they calculate little on the soil for sustenance. The lack of boldness and variety is painfully apparent in all the scenery adjacent to the coast and the water courses of North Carolina.

At 6:30 A.M. on the next day, the ships built up steam and proceeded as far as the entrance to Croatan Sound, near the marshes, but a heavy fog lay everywhere, and they were unable to navigate the channels safely and continue on to a landing site. Accordingly, the officers on board the vessels passed the remainder of the day reviewing the expedition's plan of action. Burnside spent time interviewing a young runaway slave named Thomas Robinson, who told him that Ashby's Harbor, a point several miles up the island on its western shore, would be the best place to land troops.

As evening approached on the sixth, Capt. William Parker of the Confederate States Navy paid a visit to Commodore Lynch aboard the CSS *Seabird*. He found Lynch sitting quietly in his cabin reading *Ivanhoe*. Neither officer expressed confidence that Confederates would triumph in the battle sure to occur in the morning, nor, according to Parker, "was there a naval officer in the squadron who thought we would." The topic turned to

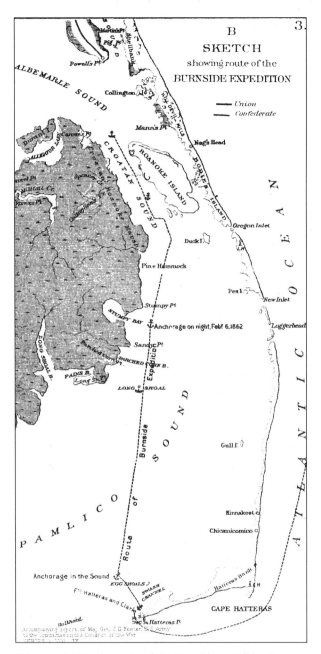

This map depicts the route of the Burnside expedition to
Roanoke Island. From *Atlas To Accompany the Official
Records of the Union and Confederate Armies*, pl. 40.

literature, and the two men talked until after midnight. Parker later thought the conversation had bordered on the absurd, having occurred so close to the impending defeat and possible death of them all.

After he returned from Richmond in early February, General Wise became ill with pneumonia. He was confined to his sickbed at the Nags Head Hotel when the U.S. flotilla arrived in Croatan Sound off Roanoke Island on February 7. As a result, command of the Confederate defenders fell to Colonel Shaw of the Eighth North Carolina Regiment.

Early on the morning of the seventh, the U.S. ships entered Croatan Sound, heading for Ashby's Harbor. The lead vessel hoisted Lord Nelson's message from a generation earlier, "This country expects every man to do his duty," to the wild cheers from the soldiers and sailors on board. Because of the narrow entrance of the sound and the marshes and swamps on both its left and right banks, Burnside's ships had to proceed in a vulnerable single file, but since the Confederates had never constructed their batteries on the southern tip of the island, passage through the strait was unopposed. As the Federal fleet moved up the sound, the Confederate gunboats formed behind the line of sunken ships and pilings. At around 9:00 A.M., the first U.S. gunboats began taking their positions off Pork Point, and at 10:30 A.M. Fort Bartow fired a signal shot, the first of the Battle of Roanoke Island.

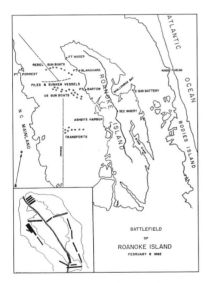

BATTLEFIELD
OF
ROANOKE ISLAND
FEBRUARY 8 1862

On February 7, 1862, the Burnside expedition arrived at Roanoke Island, and the battle for the island began. The key positions for the Federals and the defending Confederates are shown on this map, reproduced by permission. From John G. Barrett, *The Civil War in North Carolina* (Chapel Hill: University of North Carolina Press, 1963), 79.

The Federal gunboats continued to take their positions opposite the shore batteries, and at 11:45 A.M. the gunboat *Hussar* opened fire on Fort Bartow. The *Ranger, Vedette, Pioneer, Guide,* and *Picket* soon joined the assault. Most of these vessels were armed with a 30-pound Parrott gun and a 12-pound Wiard gun. Other U.S. ships concentrated their fire on the "Mosquito Fleet." Fort Bartow responded vigorously, but because of its position, it was unable to train its nine guns on the Federal ships to the south. In addition, the Confederate round shot, while striking several vessels, could not match the destructive power of the 9-inch Bormann shells used by some Federal gunners. Consequently, only one U.S. ship had to withdraw from the battle for repairs.

The naval battle continued into the afternoon, with Lynch's fleet remaining behind the obstructions in Croatan Sound. Twice the Confederate boats crossed through the line of obstacles and then quickly changed course and headed back north in an effort to lure the Federal ships into the field of fire of the northern two forts. The U.S. vessels, however, were not deceived and remained south of the obstructions, where they kept up their fire. They scored a hit on the *Curlew*, which caused her to take on water. Her captain grounded her on the western bank of the sound but in doing so blocked the aim of the battery at Fort Forrest. That battery had been firing on the enemy ships from long range but then had to cease for fear of setting the *Curlew* and the battery on fire. Lynch's fleet soon ran out of ammunition, and seeing that his boats were no match for the Union gunboats, the commodore ordered that the grounded *Curlew* and *Forrest* be destroyed, while the remainder of the fleet withdrew up the Pasquotank River to Elizabeth City to regroup and find more ammunition.

In the meantime, the Federal troop transports had been making slow progress through the channel into Croatan Sound. Around mid-afternoon the last of them anchored out of range of the Confederate guns. By that time, Burnside, who was anxious to land on Roanoke Island before nightfall, had taken the advice of the slave Thomas Robinson and a topographical engineer who earlier had reconnoitered the coastline of the island. With the information that those two supplied him, the general decided to land his troops at Ashby's Harbor, south of the Confederate forts.

The *Delaware*, under Commander Rowan, escorted the troop ships to Ashby's Harbor in order to cover the landings. Each of the transport ships had a dozen or more surfboats in tow, which were filled with soldiers. The amphibious operation required a sizable number of landing craft. To accommodate the 3,692 men in Reno's four regiments, for example, there were sixteen surfboats, five metallic rowboats, four large wooden boats, two small wooden boats, one gig, and one yawl. Sailors were kept to a minimum in each craft to make more room for the soldiers, who unfortunately for the Federals were not proficient at handling the boats. The beachhead where the troops ultimately landed was on the south side of the harbor near a structure known as the Hammond House. There the steamers moved toward the shore and cast off the surfboats when the momentum of the surf was sufficient to carry them to the beach. The first landings began at around 4:00 P.M., and within an hour nearly 4,000 men were ashore. The landing continued uncontested, and by midnight a division of 7,500 U.S. soldiers stood on the island. A battery of Dahlgren howitzers, which would later play an important role in the Federal operation, also came ashore that night. The Union gunboats further to the north had broken off their engagement with Fort Bartow at 6:30 P.M. and withdrawn to a safe anchorage for the night.

The Confederates had anticipated that the landing would take place further north near Forts Bartow, Blanchard, and Huger. When their commander, Colonel Shaw, learned that Burnside intended to put his men on the beach on the southern end of Roanoke Island, he ordered the three movable guns at the battery—blocking the causeway that connected the north and south ends of the island—moved to the sites where he thought the landings might take place. He transported the two larger pieces, an 18-pound smoothbore field gun (a Mexican War trophy) and a 24-pound navy howitzer, to the south end of Roanoke Island near a site known as Pugh's Landing. The small 6-pound field piece he had placed near Ashby's Harbor. When, however, Shaw learned that Burnside's troops would bypass Pugh's Landing and come ashore at Ashby's Harbor, he moved the three guns back to the battery straddling the causeway, where they could oppose a Union movement toward the forts. Behind the battery, he deployed 1,050 infantry.

During the night of the seventh, Burnside and Goldsborough discussed the day's events and the upcoming fight on the morrow. Goldsborough told Burnside that he was afraid to engage the rebel shore batteries again in the morning lest he inadvertently hit the Federal troops advancing up the island behind the batteries. Burnside told Goldsborough that he shared his concern and would keep the navy gunners informed of the army's positions in order to avoid any tragic mistakes.

On shore, the Union soldiers spent a wet and miserable night in the rain. One, a Private Glazier of the Twenty-third Massachusetts, wrote the following in his diary:

> Oh, how slow the time passed. How we wished our thirty and forty
> pound loads was somewhere else. Finally at 12 [midnight], we

advanced and in a few minutes set our muddy feet on the sandy cornfield where the fires were. We stacked arms, took off our equipment, and built for our company four fires of rails we took from a fence nearby. Putting on our rubber blankets to keep off the rain, which now began to come down in torrents, we sat down to the fire, took off our shoes to dry them, wrang the mud out of our pants and stockings, stirred up the fire, talked, laughed, smoked, and got smoked until morning. It was a consolation to us that our officers were obliged to take it with us, as there was only buildings enough for the field and staff [officers] of the regiments. It rained all night. It sounded quite musical as it fell on our rubber blankets while we sat around the fire.

The following morning, February 8, saw the return of fog. A boat crew from the *Delaware* landed early in the day and reconnoitered to the south and east of the Hammond House, only to find that all the rebels in that area had pulled back to the north end of the island. At 8:00 A.M. General Foster's brigade began moving north, followed by the rest of the Federal column. As the Union troops drew near the Confederate battery on the causeway, which the defenders had named Fort Defiance, they observed that the guns not only controlled the causeway but also covered a cleared field of fire in the direction of Ashby's Harbor. On each side of the causeway lay treacherous, seemingly impassable swamps. Burnside then divided his force into three segments. Five regiments commanded by Foster would attack the Confederate battery directly along the causeway. They would be supported by the six naval howitzers in the rear, which along with two regiments would hold the Federal center. With four regiments, General Reno would try to flank the Confederates through the swamp on the left of the causeway. General Parke with four regiments would attempt the same maneuver on the right.

Even with the support of the artillery pieces in their rear, Foster's troops made no progress against the effective fire from Fort Defiance. Finally after two hours, the Ninth New York Regiment—the Zouaves—commanded by Colonel Hawkins who had returned to the island, fixed bayonets and charged the rebel redoubt in a frontal assault. Although that attack was repulsed, the position was carried by the Federals when the Twenty-fifth Massachusetts Regiment finally emerged from the swamp on the left flank and part of Parke's force appeared on the right. Those flanking assaults

During the Battle of Roanoke Island, Col. Rush C. Hawkins's "Zouaves" (Ninth New York Regiment) charged the center of the Confederate defenses. Although Hawkins's troops failed to take the position, the Confederates were soon out-flanked and forced to retreat. Photograph of engraving from the State Archives.

forced the Confederates to retreat north.

Reno's brigade and the Ninth New York quickly pursued them. The New York Zouaves veered east to cut off any rebels trying to escape across Roanoke Sound to Nags Head, and in the process they captured Capt. O. J. Wise of the Richmond Blues and some of his men, as well as the two-gun battery at Midgett's Hammock. Reno's brigade had learned from a Confederate officer overtaken on the road that there were no other rebel batteries en route to the island's northern tip. Reno and his troops surged ahead. In the meantime, Parke had sent the Fourth Rhode Island and Tenth Connecticut, with one howitzer, to seize Fort Bartow, which they found deserted. Parke reported that the nine guns inside had all been spiked and the carriages wrecked before the garrison had fled.

Reno's brigade continued to press northward, led by Company E of the Twenty-first Massachusetts Regiment, commanded by Captain Bradford, who later reported that his troops came upon a large body of Confederate soldiers whom he immediately ordered to surrender. The rebels opened fire on the Federals, who responded, killing four Confederates. A

Confederate officer stepped forward under a white flag to ask for terms of surrender. He was taken to General Reno, who informed him that unconditional surrender was all that was acceptable and gave the officer time to take that message back to his commander.

The troops that had fired on the Twenty-first Massachusetts Regiment were the men of the Second Battalion North Carolina Infantry. That unit had just arrived from Norfolk on the CSS *White*. On their way south, they had passed Lynch's fleet steaming toward Elizabeth City with news of the Federal attack. Unaware that Fort Defiance had fallen and the Confederate situation was lost, the Second Battalion, commanded by Lt. Col. W. J. Green, landed and proceeded south on the island to join the battle. The shots that they fired at Captain Bradford were all that they ever fired. They had arrived just in time to surrender.

Having received Reno's message about unconditional surrender, Colonel Shaw decided that to continue to fight was useless, and he surrendered his force unconditionally. He later recalled, "with the very great disparity of forces, the moment the redoubt was flanked I considered the island lost. The struggle could have been protracted, and the small body of brave men which had been held in reserve might have been brought up into the open space to receive the fire of the overwhelming force on our flank which was under cover of trees, but they would have been sacrificed without the smallest hope of a successful [outcome]." About five hundred rebel soldiers escaped to the mainland or to Nags Head, but the rest became prisoners of war. General Wise, still ill since February 1, ordered the hotel barracks at Nags Head burned and withdrew north to Gallops Ferry and then on to Currituck, over fifteen miles to the north, just ahead of Hawkins's Zouaves, prompting Hawkins to describe him later as "a vandal and a barbarian." Fleeing North Carolina, Wise subsequently served with the army in Virginia and in the coastal defenses of South Carolina. A congressional investigation, led by Burgess S. Gaither of North Carolina, absolved him of any blame for the loss of Roanoke Island. Following the Confederate army's surrender on Roanoke Island, vessels from Goldsborough's fleet pursued Lynch's "Mosquito Fleet" to Elizabeth City, where they destroyed most of the Confederate boats and captured the town. On February 10, a Federal naval detachment raided Edenton and captured a supply of wheat and cotton.

In the Battle of Roanoke Island the Federals had lost (including 3 sailors killed and 11 wounded) 40 men killed, 225 wounded, and 13 missing. The

The victorious Federals captured approximately 2,675 Confederate prisoners on Roanoke Island. The prisoners were paroled and swore to refrain from fighting again until they had been exchanged with Union prisoners of war. Photograph of engraving from the State Archives.

Confederate losses were lighter, with 23 killed, 58 wounded, and 62 missing. In addition, the 42 guns at the forts and batteries on the island fell into Union hands. All of the rebel guns, except the three at Fort Defiance, had been spiked by the Confederates. Some had been loaded with inverted shells to explode if the guns were fired. But these efforts proved ineffectual, and all the guns were soon operational. The Federals took 2,675 prisoners, almost all of the rank and file of the regiments on the island when Shaw surrendered, and they captured 3,000 small arms of all descriptions. The Union troops also seized a number of regimental and company colors. One such flag was that of Company B of the Thirty-first North Carolina Regiment, the self-titled "OK Boys." The flag was made of heavy silk, with a white fringe. On one side was a gold brocade field with a presentation history inscribed and the unit's name in gold paint. On the other side was a Confederate first national pattern design with eleven stars and in gold paint the motto "Aut Vincere Aut More." The flag had been made by one Tempie Liles and presented to the company by the ladies of Anson County, North Carolina, at the outbreak of the war. The Twenty-first Massachusetts Regiment had accepted the surrender of Company B and thus had taken the banner as a trophy. The Twenty-sixth Massachusetts Regiment likewise

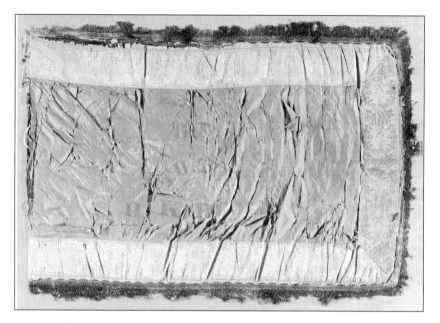

The Union troops seized a number of Confederate regimental and company flags. Among the colors captured was the flag of the "OK Boys," Company B, Thirty-first North Carolina Regiment. The Twenty-first Massachusetts Regiment took the flag. Flag in the collection of the Museum of the Confederacy, Richmond, Va. Photograph by Katherine Wetzel.

The Twenty-sixth Massachusetts Regiment captured the flag of the "Brown Mountain Boys" of Company A, Second Battalion North Carolina Infantry. Flag in the collection of the North Carolina Museum of History, Raleigh. Photograph by the museum.

captured the flag of Company A (known as the "Brown Mountain Boys"), Second Battalion North Carolina Infantry, from Stokes County.

An inspection of their prisoners and captured weapons revealed to the Federals that the Confederate defense of Roanoke Island had not been a well-planned or -equipped operation. Before the battle, a rebel soldier had written home to say that "Roanoke Island [is] a mere man trap as everyone but our leaders have long foreseen." A Federal soldier wrote home to say that only two companies of the Confederates were well uniformed and supplied—the McCullock Rangers and the Richmond Blues—with the rest in threadbare homespun clothing and carrying no two weapons that looked the same. But he added that despite their poor condition, most of the prisoners were sociable, engaging in conversation and games freely with their captors. The Thirty-first North Carolina Regiment especially was a poorly trained and equipped collection of raw farm boys. Nor had the Confederate officers themselves been confident about the fighting capabilities and morale of many of the North Carolina troops. In January Commodore Lynch had written to Secretary of the Navy Mallory, "My opinion is that North Carolina volunteers will not stand to their guns [because] men so devoid of energy are incapable of determined and long-continued resistence." One of Lynch's subordinates, Capt. Thomas Hunter, agreed with his commander and feared that coastal Carolina's soldiers might not be sufficiently loyal to the Confederate cause. Roanoke Island would be defensible, he claimed, "only so long as it is defended by troops from another state or from a more loyal part of North Carolina." General Wise noted that "the infantry were undrilled, unpaid, not sufficiently clothed and quartered, and were miserably armed with old flint muskets in bad order. In a word, the defenses were a sad farce of ignorance and neglect combined, inexcusable in any or all who were responsible for them."

Some of the captured Confederate cannons were smoothbore relics of the Mexican War. The 18-pound field piece at Fort Defiance had only 12-pound ammunition. Many of the captured rifles and muskets were either M-1832 Harper's Ferry smoothbore flintlock muskets, or War of 1812 muskets that had been hastily converted to percussion-lock mechanisms. Burnside's chief ordnance officer, D. W. Flagler, reported to the general that "some of the enemy's troops were armed with fowling pieces, sporting rifles, . . . and a motley collection of arms nearly useless for military purposes." In fact, Burnside's troops slaughtered the island livestock to feed themselves, the prisoners, and some of the locals. Furthermore, newly liberated slaves quickly pointed out where stores of food had been hidden by the local white populace.

Without the means to care for prisoners, and with no instructions to the contrary, Burnside decided to parole the Confederate captives on their honor until a possible future exchange could be worked out. Many of the captured Tar Heels were illiterate and could not sign their names to their parole forms. On February 21, 1862, five steamers carried the rebel parolees to Elizabeth City. As they disembarked, the band of the Twenty-fourth Massachusetts Regiment played a medley of musical numbers, one of which ironically was "Dixie."

4 Burnside Invades the Mainland

Following the capture of Roanoke Island, Burnside remained on the Outer Banks for about a month. During that time he attempted to establish good relations with the residents, assuring them that the Federals had their best interests at heart. On February 16, 1862, he and Goldsborough cosigned and posted a proclamation to the people of North Carolina, saying in effect that they wished to reestablish the rule of Federal law and meant no harm to the local inhabitants. They added that a few ill-intending persons had spread lies and rumors about the true intent of the U.S. expedition. Burnside personally considered the Outer Bankers to be "ignorant and inoffensive people" who had been forced to quarter the Confederate garrison out of fear for their own safety. Nearly all the remaining occupants of the island had quickly taken the oath of allegiance to the U.S. government, and Burnside saw no reason why they could not immediately return to their livelihoods, mostly fishing, which had been prevented by the Confederates for fear of fishermen falling into Union hands and providing intelligence of military value. The general authorized $2,000 to be paid to the locals in restitution for damages, and the Federals began work to improve the island's primitive roads, to build a wharf at Pork Point, and to establish telegraph lines. They also worked to renovate and strengthen the abandoned Confederate earthworks and batteries.

Burnside's first significant raid onto the mainland of North Carolina began on February 18, when a force of Hawkins's New York Zouaves and elements of the Fourth Rhode Island Regiment embarked aboard the USS *Delaware*, accompanied by the USS *Commodore Perry*, for the Hertford County town of Winton, located on the bluffs of the Chowan River. Hawkins's mission was to destroy two railroad bridges above Winton and investigate rumors of Union sentiment in the area. Realizing that Winton might become a base for the Federals to strike at the important rail junction at Weldon or at Norfolk, the Confederates hastily dispatched two companies to defend the town: the First Battalion North Carolina Infantry commanded by Lt. Col. William T. Williams and a four-gun battery commanded by Capt. J. N. Nichols. The Union force spent the night of the eighteenth at the mouth of the Chowan and on the following morning weighed anchor and proceeded up the river.

In the meantime, the Confederates had taken a position at the top of the bluff overlooking the river. Winton lay behind the bluff, and the Confederates hoped to deceive the Federals into believing that the town was undefended. They intended to lure the U.S. vessels up to the Winton wharf where Hawkins's soldiers would be unable to use their artillery and could be targeted by Confederate fire from the bluff. "For a price," a mulatto named Martha Keen agreed to entice the Federals to the dock by signaling from there that it was safe to land. But as the *Delaware* approached the dock, Colonel Hawkins, acting as a lookout in the rigging, sighted the glint of the rifles of the First North Carolina Battalion. Hawkins sounded the alarm, and the *Delaware* managed to turn short of the dock and get back to midstream and then up past Winton, where her crew turned their guns on the bluff. Meanwhile Confederate rifle and cannon fire had pierced the vessel "like a sieve," although miraculously there were no casualties.

Having silenced the Confederate artillery, the *Delaware*, with the help of the *Commodore Perry*, which had appeared, steamed downstream past the town where, along with other of Commander Rowan's vessels, it anchored for the night. The next morning the flotilla started back upstream. By the time it arrived at Winton around 10:00 A.M. on February 20, the rebels had already fled to Mount Tabor Church, several miles away. After their gunboats shelled the evacuated Confederate positions, Hawkins's men came ashore and seized Winton without a fight. Hawkins ordered buildings used for storage or occupied by Confederates to be burned. Barrels of tar were rolled into the buildings and set ablaze, and the Federal troops set about pillaging the town. In general, the Northern press praised the Winton attack, although one New York newspaper that had been soliciting contributions for the Zouaves after Roanoke Island ceased its solicitations because it was outraged at the conduct of the Union soldiers who plundered the village. But ironically the funds that the newspaper had already obtained were used to buy Colonel Hawkins a presentation sword.

Following their assault on Winton, the Union troops reembarked to continue up the Chowan to destroy railroad bridges. But they learned that the river had been obstructed upstream by Confederates. With no other route available and lacking the manpower to proceed overland, Hawkins ordered the expedition back to Roanoke Island. Burnside was neither disappointed nor discouraged by the outcome of the Winton raid. He congratulated the troops and noted the value of such raids. "The enemy is very much distracted by these frequent dashes on their coast, and seem to have but little idea where the next blow will be aimed," he declared. Perhaps if Burnside had moved faster and more vigorously in urging his troops up the Chowan to destroy the railroad bridges, he might have struck a significant blow against Confederate transportation. On the other hand, with the eventual withdrawal of Hawkins's raiding party and without sufficient troops to occupy the Confederate interior, any damage inflicted would soon have been repaired by the Confederates.

In any event, Burnside already had begun planning a much larger-scaled operation. In keeping with McClellan's original design, after the fall of Roanoke Island, Burnside turned his main attention to additional joint army/navy operations against other important sites on the North Carolina coast. His next objective would be New Bern, the state's second largest city and a vital port and commercial center located at the confluence of the Neuse and Trent Rivers. Since the beginning of the year the Confederate military had been expecting Burnside to attack New Bern, and much of the local population had already evacuated the town. Responsible for the defenses of New Bern was Confederate general L. O'B. Branch, who commanded approximately 4,000 raw troops. Hampered by a shortage of soldiers, as well as an insufficient number of tools and black laborers (local slaveholders were reluctant to allow their slaves to work on army defenses), Branch's fortifications were inadequate to defend New Bern. His chief line of defense was south of New Bern and extended from Fort Thompson, east of the town, to a swamp on the west side. Unfortunately for the Confederates, however, there was a break in the line, which existed from the left flank of the Twenty-sixth Regiment North Carolina Troops, commanded by Col. Zebulon B. Vance (who soon became governor of North Carolina), and a brick kiln located along the Atlantic and North Carolina Railroad. The rail line ran from New Bern to Morehead City. General Branch had ordered guns placed at the unguarded site, but they were not in place when Burnside's force attacked.

On March 11, 1862, General Burnside and 11,000 Federal troops, representing most of Reno's, Foster's, and Parke's brigades, boarded vessels and departed Roanoke Island for Cape Hatteras. Once at the cape, the transports became part of the larger squadron, and the troops were given last minute supplies and instructions. General Burnside announced to the troops that they were on the eve of an important event, "which could greatly demoralize the enemy and assist the Army of the Potomac in its contemplated move on Richmond." The squadron consisted of the USS

Philadelphia, USS *Stars and Stripes*, USS *Louisiana*, USS *Hetzel*, USS *Delaware*, USS *Commodore Perry*, USS *Hunchback*, USS *Southfield*, USS *Morse*, USS *Brinker*, and USS *Lockwood*, along with a number of unarmed army transport ships in tow. The fleet set sail on the morning of March 12, traveling through Pamlico Sound toward New Bern. The fleet had not been under way long before Commodore Goldsborough received orders transferring him to Hampton Roads, where the ironclad *Virginia* had attacked the Federal ships there and hampered McClellan's plan to move up the eastern Virginia peninsula toward Richmond. Goldsborough thus relinquished command in North Carolina waters to Commander Rowan.

In March 1862, Burnside attacked the port town of New Bern on the coastal mainland. The above engravings show his troops landing south of New Bern (top) and Union ships bombarding the town from the Neuse River. The troops marched northward along the banks of the Neuse to capture New Bern on March 14. Copy from the State Archives.

At about 2:00 P.M., the Union flotilla entered the mouth of the Neuse River, which was about twelve miles wide. According to historian John G. Barrett, "The river was so broad and calm that the transports, their docks crowded with uniformed men, could sail in two parallel lines. . . . Multicolored signal flags fluttering from every halyard added to the color of the occasion." Confederate obstacles in the river consisted of rows of pilings cut off just below the waterline and behind them a row of sharpened pilings with iron caps and spikes at a 45-degree angle, followed by at least thirty torpedoes with percussion caps and 200-pound gunpowder charges.

These hazards, however, did not significantly hinder the progress of the Federal boats. Around 9:00 P.M. the fleet anchored at the mouth of Slocum Creek about twelve miles below New Bern by water. At dawn on March 13, Federal gunboats began bombarding the shore at Slocum Creek in preparation for the landing of troops.

The Battle of New Bern. Photograph of engraving from the State Archives.

The bombardment proved unnecessary, for there were no Confederate defenders in the vicinity. As usual, the U.S. command had overestimated rebel defenses. A few days before the expedition got under way, Goldsborough had warned Assistant Secretary of the Navy Gustavus V. Fox that evidence suggested the presence of thousands of Confederate troops backed by a fifty-gun fortress along the banks of the river. At Slocum Creek, Burnside began disembarking his troops using the same amphibious method that he had successfully employed at Roanoke Island. Steam vessels towed troop launches toward the beach and then released them, allowing momentum to drive the barges aground. The troops then waded ashore. Having gained the beach without any resistance, the Federals began a march upriver toward New Bern. Heavy rains in the afternoon, as well as "deep sand and thick clay," made the soldiers' progress difficult. A number of miles along their march they came upon the Confederates' Croatan Works, which to their surprise they found deserted. Properly defended, those works might have posed a major obstacle to their progress.

These Confederate cotton-bale batteries defended New Bern from Union assault. The battery at top overlooks the Trent River railroad bridge burned by the retreating Confederates. Engravings from *Frank Leslie's Illustrated Newspaper*, 1862.

The troops continued their trek toward their objective until they stopped near the Fort Thompson line to camp for the night. They spent a miserable evening huddled around fires, trying to stay warm in the pouring rain. But by early morning on the fourteenth, Burnside had his men up and moving in preparation for advance on the rebel line. For the attack, he divided his force into three columns. General Foster and his contingent took a position on the Federal right, between the river and the railroad. General

Reno's column occupied the ground on the left of the railroad. General Parke's force stood in reserve along the rail line, where it might come to the aid of either Foster or Reno.

The Confederates had taken their positions in anticipation of the assault. On the defensive line, from left to right beginning at Fort Thompson stood the Twenty-seventh Regiment North Carolina Troops, the Thirty-seventh North Carolina, the Seventh North Carolina, and the Thirty-fifth North Carolina. Next came the old brick kiln. To defend the vulnerable gap near that site, Branch made the mistake of placing a raw militia battalion, poorly trained, equipped, and armed. On the other side of the brickyard, Vance's Twenty-sixth Regiment waited, supported by an "independent company" and two dismounted cavalry companies. Branch held in reserve the Thirty-third North Carolina. Two field artillery pieces guarded the right side of the railroad, and ten supported the infantry on the left.

Foster's column made first contact on the Confederate left at Fort Thompson, but several successive charges were repulsed by the three light guns from the fort. The Federal gunboats bombarded the rebel earthworks as the Federals advanced, but poor aiming by the naval gunners resulted in a number of casualties in Foster's advance companies. Despite the volume of enemy fire, the arrival of reinforcements, and repeated assaults, the fort and the Confederate left remained firm.

But then several companies of Reno's column discovered the weakly held Confederate militia position at the brick kiln. Reno's troops charged through the position, turned right, and began leveling a deadly fire into the flank of the militia, who began to run. The retreating militia excited panic in the Thirty-fifth North Carolina, who also began to flee to the rear. Hurriedly, Branch ordered the Thirty-third North Carolina forward to seal the break, which was accomplished after a bayonet charge and bloody hand-to-hand fighting with the Federals who had penetrated the line. In the process, however, the Thirty-third North Carolina became disorganized, and General Parke ordered his brigade to attack the weak point at the kiln. His assault was successful in piercing the rebel line. His troops poured through the break, and this time there were no reserves on which to call. Foster, realizing that the Confederates were in trouble, ordered another frontal assault on Fort Thompson, hoping to capitalize on Parke's successful attack. This time Foster's maneuver succeeded and the Confederate line began to crumble. A pincer movement by Parke and Foster sent the rebels into a disorganized retreat toward town.

Burnside's troops crossing the Trent River at the burned railroad bridge. Engraving from *Frank Leslie's Illustrated Newspaper*, 1862.

Only the Confederate far left held onto its position. Vance's Twenty-sixth Regiment fought a successful withdrawal into the swamps for over an hour, thus keeping the enemy at bay. It then navigated the seventy-five yards across Brice's Creek under Federal fire. The other Confederate regiments were not so fortunate. In the course of retreating across the Trent River into New Bern, the panicking men set fire to the bridge, and thus a large number of troops were stranded on the eastern bank and captured. Branch ordered the men who did reach the town to regroup along with the Twenty-sixth North Carolina at Kinston, a town some miles to the west. As the Confederates fled, the Union gunboats began shelling suspected Confederate positions within New Bern, but that soon halted when the U.S. troops crossed the Trent and entered the town. During the battle, 165 Confederate soldiers were killed or wounded and over 400 captured. Northern losses were 470 killed or wounded.

Although there was some destruction of New Bern by Burnside's assault, the town for the most part remained intact. Initially looting by soldiers and slaves occurred until a provost marshal established order. Burnside strongly garrisoned the town and posted guards for those inhabitants who

CHAPTER FOUR

A view of New Bern from the opposite bank of the Neuse River. From this site, the U.S. flagship *Delaware* transported Federal troops across to the town. Photograph of engraving from the State Archives.

required protection. Some residents, of course, had already fled the town prior to the battle. The Federals soon began work on defenses to thwart any counterattacks. The Union army occupied New Bern for the rest of the war, and it proved an effective headquarters for U.S. operations in eastern North Carolina.

North Carolinians and the War Department in Richmond were alarmed and outraged at the fall of New Bern. The state's inhabitants were frightened at having the "Yankees" so close to their homes and livelihoods. Confederate authorities feared that from New Bern a "successful sweep of Burnside's army across North Carolina 'would divide the upper Confederacy.'" Gen. Robert E. Lee wrote to President Jefferson Davis that another such disaster in North Carolina "would be ruinous." In order to prevent such an event the War Department removed General Gatlin from command of the Department of North Carolina and replaced him with Gen. Theophilus H. Holmes. Gen. Samuel G. French replaced General Anderson at Wilmington. In an effort to protect its native soil, the State of North Carolina persuaded the War Department to transfer an infantry brigade, led by one of its native sons, Gen. Robert Ransom Jr., from Virginia to east-

Having captured New Bern, Union soldiers occupied many buildings in the town. This dwelling, the Isaac Taylor House on Craven Street, served as headquarters for the Forty-fifth Regiment Massachusetts Infantry. Photograph from the U.S. Army Military History Institute, Carlisle, Pennsylvania.

ern North Carolina. He would rejoin the Army of Northern Virginia in June 1862. Holmes organized his forces into four brigades and stationed the bulk of them near Goldsboro in anticipation of Burnside moving further inland.

Burnside, however, had other plans and was contemplating capturing Fort Macon, which stood on the eastern tip of Bogue Banks near the towns of Beaufort and Morehead City. The fort guarded Beaufort Inlet, the only inlet on the Outer Banks still open to Confederate shipping. Burnside reasoned that before he could strike further into the interior or eventually move against Wilmington to the south, he had to take this fort in his rear. In preparation for such an attack, he ordered General Parke to occupy Morehead City and Beaufort. After establishing his troops in Beaufort by

This building on lower Craven Street served as part of the "Quartermaster Department" of New Bern and held supplies for the Federal army. Photograph from the U.S. Army Military History Institute.

March 23, Parke contacted the Union blockading fleet and began making plans for capturing Fort Macon.

In the meantime, however, word had reached Burnside that the Confederates were building ironclads at Norfolk and intended to transport them into the Albemarle region through the Dismal Swamp and Albemarle and Chesapeake canals. Burnside then dispatched Reno to move from New Bern to South Mills on the Dismal Swamp canal, destroy the lock at that site, and then "proceed up the head of Currituck [Albemarle and Chesapeake] Canal and blow in its banks." Reno's contingent of the Twenty-first and Fifty-first Massachusetts Regiments was joined en route by Col. Rush Hawkins and three regiments from Roanoke Island: the Ninth New York, Eighty-ninth New York, and Sixth New Hampshire. On April 19, just below South Mills, Reno's force encountered Col. A. R. Wright and the Third Georgia Regiment, which earlier had served in the defense of Hatteras. Wright also had under his command most of a brigade of North Carolina militia. Wright's troops beat off two charges by Reno's men before retiring "in good order." Reno did not pursue but fled back to New Bern via Elizabeth

The Federals established a number of outlying fortifications and camps in the New Bern vicinity. The blockhouse at top was constructed at Evans Mill across the Trent River from the town. Below are the log huts of "Grove Camp". for the Twenty-fifth Massachusetts Regiment and the Third Regiment New York Cavalry. Photographs from the U.S. Army Military History Institute.

City, leaving behind his dead and wounded to be cared for by assistant surgeon Orrin Warren. The Federals arrived back in New Bern on April 22. Their casualties totaled thirteen killed and 101 wounded. Wright's losses were six killed and nineteen wounded. Because Reno failed to obstruct the

CHAPTER FOUR

The U.S. Army occupied New Bern and the surrounding area for the rest of the war. These Champney drawings depict Union sentries at a railroad bridge near the town and at nearby Camp Pierson. From the Outer Banks History Center.

canals, the battle at South Mills has been regarded as a Confederate victory.

While Reno's expedition was ongoing, Parke continued his plans for capturing Fort Macon. From his headquarters at Carolina City, near Morehead City, he sent a request to the fort for its surrender. The commanding officer, Lt. Col. Moses J. White, refused, and Parke began his plans to take the citadel. On March 29 a landing party of twenty men, protected by the guns of a U.S. warship, established a preliminary beachhead on Bogue Banks. That toehold began the movement of troops, guns, and supplies onto the island for the assault on Fort Macon. By March 31, two companies of the Eighth Regiment Connecticut Infantry had established a firm beach-

Union soldiers "in quarters" at Fort Spinola, across the Trent River, south
of New Bern. Champney drawing from the Outer Banks History Center.

head and a camp about eight miles from the fort. This detachment was
soon joined by eight companies of the Fourth Regiment Rhode Island
Infantry, five additional companies of the Eighth Connecticut, the Fifth
Rhode Island, one company of the First Regiment United States Artillery,
and one company of the Third Regiment New York Light Artillery. Parke
transported men, supplies, and artillery from Carolina City to Bogue Banks
aboard various steamers, scows, schooners, and rafts.

Meanwhile the Confederate garrison was making its own plans to defend
the fort. The U.S. government had built the fort in 1825 to guard Beaufort
harbor. It had been designed for fifty-six guns, but only four 24-pound
smoothbores were in place at the outbreak of the Civil War. As only a few
soldiers and a caretaker sergeant had been on duty at the site prior to 1861,
the installation itself began to crumble and decay. Its masonry was crack-
ing, its two hot-shot furnaces needed complete rebuilding, many of its
cannons had been left lying in the sand, its casemates needed painting and
plastering, and much of its woodwork had rotted. After the Confederates
seized the fort on April 14, 1861, they immediately began to work on reno-
vations, including extensive repairs on the walls and foundation. By
September twenty-one guns had been mounted, and by December thirty-
six guns were in place. But a large number still lay in the sand. Much still
remained to be done in the spring of 1862. The fort had only three hundred

CHAPTER FOUR

effective soldiers with which to defend itself. Mumps and pneumonia had also weakened the garrison. Sand dunes remained all around the fort, never having been leveled, providing cover for any enemy assault. The defenders lacked sufficient powder and ammunition. There was not an experienced artillery officer among the garrison, nor a single rifled cannon or mortar. Someone thought of elevating the smoothbore cannon to unnatural angles to provide makeshift mortars, but that idea was soon abandoned. Furthermore, the smoothbore guns could not reach ships over a mile offshore. British officers who once had visited Beaufort and inspected the fort had pronounced it indefensible.

Nevertheless, Colonel White and his men made what preparations they could for the impending Federal assault. They demolished side buildings, burned boats at the dock, tarred sand bags, and held gun drill every day, although they conserved their powder by firing only a few rounds at the U.S. warships. Capt. Stephen D. Pool of the First North Carolina Artillery manned a picket station three miles from the fort, and from the station he relayed information to Colonel White.

On April 8, small-scale fighting took place between Union troops and the rebels. Further skirmishes followed on the ninth and tenth. On the eleventh, Parke ordered a reconnaissance in force toward the fort. His troops pushed to within one mile of the fort as the Confederate pickets retreated. Then fire from the fort halted their advance, but the Federals held their position until their officers could select sites for artillery and then withdrew under the protection of the guns of the offshore fleet. In the next few days, Parke's men labored around the clock to push forward rifle pits and batteries. Under the cover of darkness, they managed to establish three batteries, hidden by sand dunes, about 1,300 yards from the fort. They dug rifle pits about 2,000 feet away. Attempts to get closer were thwarted by gunfire from White's cannon. As the U.S. troops continued their efforts, the Confederates kept up a constant but largely ineffectual shelling. By mid-April the fort was cut off from all communication with the outside. During the siege, the Confederate soldiers almost mutinied over the issue of flour rations.

On April 23, under a flag of truce, a U.S. officer presented to Colonel White Parke's second demand for surrender. Although White refused, he did request a conference to discuss terms. On the following day he met with Burnside, who had been directing operations from aboard his flag-ship the *Mary Price*, on nearby Shackleford Banks. Nothing was resolved at

Fort Macon

From railroad leading to Wharf.

Following the capture of New Bern, Burnside's army attacked Fort Macon, which guarded Beaufort's harbor and fell to the Federals on April 25, 1862. Champney made these drawings during the subsequent Union occupation of the fort. From the Outer Banks History Center.

the meeting, and both sides prepared for more fighting.

Firing between the fort and the Federal batteries resumed on the morning of the twenty-fifth. Initially, much of it was ineffective, particularly for White's troops, who without mortars to lob shells, could do little damage to the Union positions. The U.S. fleet entered the fray late, and around 8:30 A.M. the steamers *Ellis*, *State of Georgia*, *Chippewa*, and *Gunsbak* commenced firing at the fort. Fort Macon, being designed specifically for seaborne attacks, easily fought the Federal ships to a standstill within an hour. The accuracy of the fort's response and rough weather forced the vessels to

The guard room at Fort Macon. Champney drawing from the Outer Banks History Center.

retire. But the Federal land batteries continued to shell their target, and as their aim improved, their fire became amazingly accurate. Of the approximately 1,150 shots fired, about 560 hit the fort. In the afternoon "every shot fired from [the Federal] batteries fell in or near" the fort. The Union artillery disabled a total of nineteen Confederate guns. Lt. W. S. Andrews, the U.S. signal officer at Beaufort, was primarily responsible for such marksmanship. From Beaufort, Andrews observed where the shells were landing, and he used signal flags to direct corrections to the batteries on Bogue Banks.

Realizing the futility of holding out under such an accurate and devastating bombardment, Colonel White ran up a white flag, and all firing ceased. White then dispatched two officers to confer with General Parke. Parke stated that only an unconditional surrender would be acceptable. When the Confederate officers refused those terms, Parke suggested that the truce remain in effect overnight to give him time to discuss the situation with Burnside aboard the *Mary Price*. After considering the matter, Burnside ordered two officers ashore to inform White of the terms of surrender. The terms were that the fort and all its men and arms would sur-

Barracks at Fort Macon. Champney drawing from the Outer Banks History Center.

render, and the captured officers and men would be released on their honor not to fight again until properly exchanged as prisoners of war and would return to their homes, taking with them their private property. White accepted Burnside's terms and then went aboard the *Mary Price* to sign the surrender papers. Both commanding officers then went ashore for the surrender ceremony at the fort. Casualties on both sides had been light. The Confederates had lost eight killed and twenty wounded, and the Federals suffered one killed and two wounded. The victors seized intact the fort and all its weapons, as well as two blockade-runners moored nearby. Burnside wasted no time in paroling his prisoners. On the twenty-sixth his flagship steamed back to New Bern, where the general's soldiers and staff acknowledged his triumph with enthusiastic congratulations. With the fall of Fort Macon and the closing of Beaufort's harbor, only the port of Wilmington, guarded by Fort Fisher, remained open to blockade-running on the North Carolina coast.

Having seized Fort Macon, Burnside had achieved his first three objectives as specified in McClellan's orders of January 7: Roanoke Island, New Bern, and the port of Beaufort. He then turned his attention to the other

CHAPTER FOUR

parts of the army's plan for North Carolina. That is, a strike inland toward Goldsboro and Raleigh, and then an assault on the blockade-running port of Wilmington. To launch such a campaign, however, he believed that he needed more troops and supplies. Since arriving in the Tar Heel State, he had acquired a force of 17,000 men, but he remained convinced that he would need more if he were to carry out a further invasion. The War Department, however, soon informed him that it had no more troops to spare him. He was also hindered in effecting his plans by orders from McClellan to coordinate his movements with McClellan's Peninsula Campaign in Virginia. Since March, McClellan had landed an amphibious force of the Army of the Potomac on the peninsula between the York and James Rivers and was moving toward Richmond. On April 2, McClellan, an extremely cautious tactician, had written to Burnside tentatively urging him to move toward Goldsboro. "Great caution will, however, be necessary," declared McClellan, "as the enemy might throw large forces in that direction. . . . [It] would not do for you to be caught. We cannot afford any reverse at present." Timid in his movement up the Virginia peninsula, McClellan soon halted his expedition before Yorktown and began a siege. He instructed Burnside not to move into the North Carolina interior until the outcome of Yorktown had been determined.

By May 4, McClellan's troops had forced a Confederate evacuation of Yorktown and renewed their trek toward Richmond. But the commander of the Army of the Potomac, although still desirous of cooperating with Burnside, gave the general no specific orders or deadline for advancing into the interior of North Carolina. On his own volition, however, Burnside authorized two coastal expeditions from his headquarters at New Bern. Already, shortly after the fall of New Bern in March, he had dispatched three gunboats (the *Delaware*, *Louisiana*, and *Commodore Perry*) and the troop transport *Admiral*, carrying the Twenty-fourth Massachusetts Regiment, to the town of Washington, north of New Bern on the Tar-Pamlico River. Landing at Washington without meeting any resistance, the Federals found that the town had been abandoned by the Confederate defenders, who had retreated up the Tar River toward Greenville. Many of the civilians loyal to the Confederacy had also fled. But the significant Union sentiment among those citizens who remained persuaded Burnside to occupy the town with a company of the Twenty-fourth Regiment and several gunboats to protect any inhabitants who professed allegiance to the United States.

Alarmed at the Federal success in coastal North Carolina, Gov. Zebulon

Wharf at Fort Macon. Champney drawing from the Outer Banks History Center.

B. Vance wrote to the Confederate secretary of war James A. Seddon on April 28 to express his displeasure at the lack of attention that the War Department was giving to the Tar Heel State. "From Roanoke Island to the late siege of Washing[ton]," Vance declared, "the history of the War has been a succession of calamities in North Carolina. . . . I shall not pretend to say that our defence is intentionally neglected, but that it is very poorly provided for is a fact too patent to deny."

Then in early May, U.S. Navy gunboats arrived at the town of Plymouth on the Roanoke River. Finding it undefended by Confederate soldiers, the sailors left a copy of Burnside's and Goldsborough's proclamation and departed. On May 14, three U.S. gunboats again called at Plymouth before pushing upriver to capture the Confederate steamer *Alice* just below Williamston. After also stopping at Windsor on the Cashie River, the flotilla returned to Plymouth, where Commander Rowan ordered them to remain to protect the Unionists there. In June a company of the Ninth New York Regiment joined the navy in occupying the Roanoke River town.

Between April 7 and June 5, Burnside's troops fought a number of skirmishes in the Coastal Plain. Those included clashes at Newport in Carteret County, Gillett's Farm in Onslow County, Haughton's Mill near Trenton in

Jones County, and Tranter's Creek in Martin County. Then on June 25, the general received orders from McClellan to advance on Goldsboro in full force. But just as he began moving his troops forward, utilizing two locomotives with fifty cars and a large wagon train, he received a message from President Lincoln ordering him to leave North Carolina and reinforce McClellan, who was fleeing back down the peninsula, pursued by Gen. Robert E. Lee's Army of Northern Virginia in the Seven Days Campaign of June 25-July 1, 1862. (Lee had taken charge of the defense of Richmond when the original commander of the Confederate defenders, Gen. Joseph E. Johnston, had been wounded at the Battle of Seven Pines on May 31, 1862.)

Burnside departed North Carolina on July 6 with seven thousand troops to reinforce McClellan on the peninsula. Gen. John G. Foster then assumed command of the Department of North Carolina, which now included over nine thousand men. Lee's attack on McClellan forced the Federals' withdrawal to Harrison Landing on the James River, from which the Union general would eventually evacuate his force from the peninsula. The Army of Northern Virginia's victory over McClellan's Army of the Potomac was significant. But, according to historian John G. Barrett, "it must be balanced against General Burnside's victories in eastern North Carolina." Barrett maintains that the "Federal operations in North Carolina were far greater than [Confederate] authorities ever anticipated." The Federal presence in coastal North Carolina would continue to plague the Confederates for the rest of the war. Not only had all the state's blockade-running ports except Wilmington been closed, but as long as the U.S. troops held bases at New Bern and other coastal locations, Confederate units that were sorely needed in Virginia would have to be detailed from Lee's army to help contain the Federals. Furthermore, any time that the Confederate army in Virginia planned an offensive, it had to consider "the possibility of a counterstrike from the easily enlargeable army . . . behind the fortifications of New Bern and within a few hours by open sea of the Confederate capital." The Federal presence in the Coastal Plain of the Tar Heel State also denied Lee's army many foodstuffs and other supplies from that rich agricultural region.

After joining McClellan in Virginia, Burnside did not return to North Carolina but continued to serve with the Army of the Potomac and took command of that army following the Battle of Antietam in September 1862. He eventually lost that command as the result of a disastrous tactical blunder and defeat at the Battle of Fredericksburg in December 1862.

Despite the damage that the fiasco at Fredericksburg did to his later reputation, he nevertheless had campaigned successfully in North Carolina and left his mark on the conduct of the war.

5 John G. Foster Raids the Interior

After Burnside departed North Carolina, Gen. John G. Foster had to forgo plans to attack Goldsboro. The absence of the two divisions that his predecessor had taken with him to Virginia left Foster with an insufficient number of troops to conduct the strike inland. But as a capable engineer, he set about perfecting the fortifications protecting New Bern. Using his soldiers and slaves who had escaped to Union lines, he had turned his base of operations into a formidable fortress by the end of the summer. West of New Bern, earthworks extended from the Trent to the Neuse River. Included in that line of defense were Fort Totten on the Federal left, Fort Rowan in the center, and Fort Dutton on the far right. An armored train left New Bern daily to patrol along the Atlantic and North Carolina Railroad. Within a short period, New Bern boasted defenses that gave it security second only to Fort Monroe as a Federal outpost.

Gen. John G. Foster succeeded Burnside as commander of U.S. troops in coastal North Carolina. Photograph of engraving from the State Archives.

The Federals, however, did not cower behind their fortifications. In July Commander Rowan ordered a naval expedition under the command of Lt. C. W. Flusser to travel up the Roanoke River to determine if the Confederates were fortifying the riverbanks or building gunboats at the towns along the river. Flusser's three gunboats managed to run past intense gunfire from Confederate cavalry on the tall bluff of Rainbow Heights and reach Hamilton in Martin County, where the Federals captured a steamer and occupied the town for a short time.

Foster ordered a number of other raids to reconnoiter, scout, and disrupt Confederate activity. The Twenty-seventh and Seventeenth Massachusetts Regiments moved by separate routes to Pollocksville on the Trent River and engaged the enemy at several points within a fifty-mile circuit. Other raiding parties scouted the area south of New Bern and the regions around

Washington, Plymouth, and Greenville. Foster personally led a force of five thousand men on a raid of the town of Tarboro, located upstream on the Tar River. The purpose of the raid was to capture three Confederate regiments operating and gathering supplies in the inner Coastal Plain. Beginning their march from Washington on the morning of October 31, 1862, the expedition, which included the newly formed Forty-fourth Regiment Massachusetts Infantry, encountered Confederate resistance late in the afternoon at Little Creek about six miles from Williamston. Although they were mostly raw recruits with no combat experience, Foster's men drove the Confederates to Rawls's Mill about a mile further away. At that site the Federals forced their adversaries out of their works and across a bridge, which the fleeing Confederates burned behind them. During the night, U.S. engineers repaired the bridge, and on the next morning Foster's men entered Williamston, which, upon finding it mostly deserted, they began to plunder. On the next day, they proceeded to the abandoned Confederate position at Rainbow Banks on the Roanoke River. They then marched three miles into the town of Hamilton, which also was practically deserted. Despite Foster's prohibitive orders, his troops pillaged the town, destroying property and setting a number of buildings on fire. On November 5, they drew within a few miles of Tarboro, but they did not pursue the retreating troops into the town. Instead, they quickly withdrew when they received reports that many Confederate reinforcements were soon to arrive by rail. Within a week Foster's raiding party had returned to its base in New Bern. The Tarboro raid did not achieve a great deal other than the liberation of a large number of slaves. The raiders destroyed considerable private property but captured only five prisoners.

On November 23 the USS *Ellis*, commanded by Lt. William B. Cushing, launched a raid up the New River from the inlet below Bogue Banks to capture any Confederate vessels, as well as the town of Jacksonville, in Onslow County, and destroy any enemy saltworks. Cushing accomplished his mission, but on the way back to the New River Inlet, he ran his gunboat aground. He stripped the *Ellis* of valuables and placed most of his crew aboard captured vessels and sent them back to the safety of the inlet and open water. He and six volunteers remained behind, and they barely escaped in a small boat when Confederates on the banks of the river opened fire. Having lost his ship, Cushing expected a court of inquiry, but instead the navy commended him for his actions.

The Confederates in the eastern counties staged some raids of their own.

On September 6, a raid led by Col. Stephen D. Pool surprised the U.S. garrison at Washington. The attack force consisted of units from the Seventeenth (Second Organization), Fifty-fifth, and Eighth North Carolina infantry regiments and a detachment from the First Regiment North Carolina Artillery acting as infantry. Under cover of fog, Pool's men surprised the Federal troops in Washington. Fighting ensued in the streets until the fog lifted, and the U.S. gunboats *Picket* and *Louisiana* began firing on the attackers. The tide turned briefly back to the Confederates when the magazine aboard the *Picket* exploded, killing the captain and nineteen crewmen. But Federal reinforcements—the First Regiment North Carolina Union Volunteers, commanded by Col. Edward E. Potter—eventually drove off Pool and his raiders.

Confederate raiders struck again in December, this time at Plymouth, garrisoned by a small contingent of U.S. troops. The attack, led by Col. John Lamb—commanding several companies of the Seventeenth North Carolina, a squadron of cavalry, and an artillery battery—surprised the Federals, who, nevertheless, had time to form a line across Main Street. Screaming the "Rebel Yell," the Confederate cavalry charged the line. The Yankee soldiers fired a volley and then ran away. Lamb then ordered his artillery to bombard the *Southfield*, the only gunboat at Plymouth at the time. Disabled by Lamb's artillery, the vessel withdrew downriver. The garrison's commander, Capt. Barnabas Ewer, also fled, abandoning his men as he took refuge aboard the *Southfield*. The raiders then burned a large portion of the town, including the Union headquarters and its records, before retreating.

Such Confederate counterattacks, however, did not result in major harm to Federal outposts or impede Foster's plans to strike into the interior. Since Burnside's departure, the number of Federal troops at New Bern and environs had been growing. By December 1862 Foster had almost twice the men he had when Burnside left for Virginia with seven thousand soldiers. He soon began making plans for an attack on the interior of North Carolina to coincide with the upcoming attack of the Army of the Potomac, then commanded by Burnside, on Fredericksburg, Virginia. Foster's assignment was to move on Goldsboro and there to destroy the Wilmington and Weldon Railroad bridge over the Neuse River. On December 11, his force marched out of New Bern. The column included 10,000 infantry, 40 pieces of artillery, and 640 cavalry. The expedition met with little resistance until it arrived at Southwest Creek near Kinston. At that site, the Confederates had destroyed the bridge and stationed troops supported by artillery on the opposite bank. Unfortunately for Foster's soldiers, the creek was not easily fordable at that point, so the general ordered the Ninth New Jersey and the Eighty-fifth Pennsylvania to get across somehow and turn the Confederate flank. By various means, including floating on debris and swimming, the two regiments reached the other side and drove off the enemy. By that time, Gen. Nathan G. ("Shanks") Evans had assumed command of the Confederates and ordered them to retire to the Neuse River. There his men, who belonged to both North Carolina and South Carolina units, dug in about two miles from the bridge at Kinston. The South Carolinians were on the Confederate left and the North Carolinians on the right.

At around 9:00 A.M. on December 14, Foster's troops attacked, with the Ninth New Jersey in the lead as skirmishers. As the assault progressed, the Federals managed to turn the Confederate left, forcing the South Carolinians to fall back across the bridge. The center and right of Evans's line, however, did not receive orders to withdraw. Evans, thinking that all his force had retired across the bridge, then ordered his artillery to shell the Confederate position. That fire, combined with the Federal onslaught, forced the line of defense to give way. The retreating troops panicked when they saw the bridge that they were to cross had been set ablaze. Many made a mad dash to get across, and about four hundred trapped on the other side were captured by the oncoming Federals, who soon put out the fire.

Evans rallied his men and re-formed a line about two miles beyond Kinston. Foster pursued and sent a message to Evans demanding his surrender. Evans responded to the Union messenger: "Tell your General to go to hell." Foster decided against continuing the attack that day and encamped for the night near the town. During the evening, he learned that Lee's army had defeated the Army of the Potomac at Fredericksburg and Confederate reinforcements were on their way to North Carolina. Despite his concern that Burnside had been defeated and Evans might be reinforced, Foster decided to move on to Goldsboro and do as much damage to the railroad as possible before withdrawing back to New Bern. On the morning of the fifteenth, his regiments crossed back over the Neuse River and began a march along the river road toward Goldsboro.

The Federals halted on the evening of December 15 a few miles from Whitehall, a village south of the Neuse River and eighteen miles below Goldsboro. Foster sent two companies of cavalry and a number of cannons toward Whitehall. That detachment clashed with the Confederates and even used a bonfire of barrels of turpentine to light their attack, but it failed to prevent the Confederates from burning the bridge over the Neuse. On the following morning the main U.S. column arrived at Whitehall. There Foster determined to engage the enemy across the river as if he meant to recapture the area and rebuild the bridge. But he intended to break off the fight and continue to Goldsboro along the main road. After a heated duel in which the Federals suffered a significant number of casualties but carried the day with their artillery, Foster ordered his column to march on to Goldsboro.

Confederate general Thomas L. Clingman defended against a raid by Foster near Goldsboro in December 1862. Following that clash, Foster ordered his troops back to New Bern. Photograph from the State Archives.

On the morning of the seventeenth, the Union troops reached the Wilmington and Weldon Railroad, and Foster ordered some of his cavalry to Dudley Station and Everittsville, just below Goldsboro, to destroy railroad property. He also commanded five of his regiments to advance down the track toward Goldsboro and burn the railroad bridge over the Neuse River. The troops of Gen. Thomas L. Clingman guarded the bridge, and Confederate artillery covered the site from a hill close by. After two hours of fierce fighting, the Union troops reached a point near enough to the bridge that a soldier succeeded in running forward and setting fire to the structure. With the bridge burned, Foster ordered his troops back to New Bern.

The Federal raid on Goldsboro had been only a partial success. News of Burnside's defeat at Fredericksburg encouraged Foster to move fast on his raid and return to his base at New Bern as quickly as possible, lest he be caught outside his defenses by Confederate reinforcements from Virginia. His men did manage to devastate the countryside in a portion of eastern North Carolina. They ransacked Kinston and, to some extent, terrorized the local populace in the Coastal Plain. But the success of their main mission, to disrupt the operation of the Wilmington and Weldon Railroad, was fleeting. Whatever damage

Foster's raid did to the track and equipment was merely superficial. The Confederates quickly rebuilt the bridge at Goldsboro, and the railroad was back in operation within two weeks. Nevertheless, the coastal Federal forces continued to launch interior raids, perhaps the most notable of which was that led by Brig. Gen. Edward E. Potter (recently promoted from colonel) on Greenville, Tarboro, and Rocky Mount in July 1863.

6 Efforts for Wartime Reconstruction and Reunion

Perhaps one of the strangest, and certainly most overlooked, episodes of the Civil War in North Carolina was the Federal government's attempts to establish a Unionist government in the state while the conflict was ongoing. At the outset of the war, President Abraham Lincoln believed that a majority of the inhabitants in the newly created Confederacy, with the exception of South Carolina, had remained loyal to the Union even after their states had seceded. Lincoln hoped that as U.S. troops penetrated into the South—as they did in coastal North Carolina—the residents who were still loyal to the Union would aid the invading Federal troops, accept a wartime reconstruction program, and lead their states back into the Union. Consequently, North Carolina was one of four Confederate states (Arkansas, Louisiana, and Tennessee were the other three) in which Lincoln appointed military governors in 1862. Among those four states, writes Lincoln scholar William C. Harris, "The North Carolina experiment created the greatest controversy, and its failure was one reason why Lincoln came to have second thoughts about southern Unionist strength and its corollary, the early restoration of civil rule in the rebel states."

Shortly after General Butler's landing at Cape Hatteras in 1861, Charles Henry Foster, a newspaper editor from Murfreesboro in Hertford County, North Carolina, appeared in Washington, D.C., and asked for an interview with the president. He asked Lincoln for recognition as the leader of North Carolina's Unionists. He also brought with him to present before the U.S. House Committee of Elections the contrived results of a bogus Unionist election giving him a seat in the U.S. Congress. He claimed that there were thousands of Union sympathizers in North Carolina, and he sought Lincoln's authorization to raise a brigade of North Carolinians to fight for the Union. Denied his dubious seat in Congress and without any authorization from the president, Foster returned to North Carolina, where he would continue his efforts to develop a rump Unionist government and have himself elected to Congress. Lincoln had dismissed Foster's overture primarily because he considered it premature. The Federals only held Hatteras at that time, with no substantial foothold on the mainland of North Carolina. Lincoln also probably had heard of the low opinion of Foster that had come from Benjamin Hedrick, an employee in Salmon P.

Chase's Treasury Department. Hedrick was an antislavery advocate and Republican who had been dismissed from his professorship at the University of North Carolina and run out of the Tar Heel State. Hedrick maintained that Foster was "an unmitigated humbug and cheat," who

New England native and Murfreesboro newspaper editor Charles Henry Foster attempted and failed to organize a loyal Unionist government in coastal North Carolina during the war. Photograph from the Foster Papers, Southern Historical Collection, Wilson Library, University of North Carolina at Chapel Hill.

CHAPTER SIX

could not be trusted to lead North Carolina back into the Union. Nevertheless, Lincoln did not discourage Foster from continuing the promotion of Unionism.

Foster had been born in Orono, Maine, in 1830. He graduated with high honors from Bowdoin College in 1855. He then read law with Israel Washburn, later governor of Maine, and was admitted to the bar in 1856. But he soon rejected law for a career in journalism. Having campaigned for the presidential election of Democrat James Buchanan, he became editor in 1857 of the Democratic southern-rights newspaper the *Southern Statesman* in Norfolk, Virginia. Shortly thereafter he moved to the larger Norfolk *Day Book*, where he was assistant editor. In the following year he served as a delegate to the Democratic state convention in Petersburg and published some essays and poetry in several periodicals. In 1859 he moved to Murfreesboro and purchased the *Citizen*, a Democratic weekly. In the columns of his newspaper, he referred to himself as "a southern man permanently identified with the institutions of the South." He even joined the Knights of the Golden Circle, a pro-slavery territorial organization that pledged in its charter to "defend Constitutional rights and to espouse the cause of the South against the North in the event of a section collision." He soon married Susan A. Carter of Murfreesboro. During the national election of 1860, he was elected an alternate to the Democratic convention in Charleston, which adjourned without a nominee. He subsequently served as a delegate from North Carolina in the Southern Democrats' Baltimore convention, where he supported the presidential candidacy of John C. Breckinridge.

In 1860, as the Buchanan administration left office, Foster sold the *Citizen* and sought a position with the Post Office Department. He also ran as a delegate to the February 1861 state convention to consider the question of secession. During that time his political views and loyalties changed. He then renounced his pro-southern bias and became a strong proponent of the Union, opposed to secession. He abandoned his campaign for the secession convention and left for Washington, D.C., to accept a clerkship with the Post Office Department. William N. H. Smith, a former U.S. congressman and future Confederate congressman and chief justice of the North Carolina Supreme Court, substituted for Foster in the February convention. Returning from Washington to Murfreesboro for a visit in May, Foster came under charges by some local residents that he was a spy for Lincoln, and he fled the town, leaving behind his wife and baby.

Arriving in Washington, D.C., he failed in an attempt to secure a seat as

North Carolina's Unionist representative in a special session of Congress in July 1861. He then disappeared for two months before he returned to Washington, again bearing bogus North Carolina Unionist credentials to Congress and seeking an audience with Lincoln.

After Lincoln's rejection, Foster, failing in his second phony bid for Congress, did not give up on his efforts to form a Unionist government in North Carolina. To promote his congressional candidacy and Unionism in coastal North Carolina, Foster had the assistance of Rev. Marble Nash Taylor, a native Virginian missionary who had been assigned to Cape Hatteras by the North Carolina Methodist Conference on December 11, 1860. As early as September 1861, Taylor was actively speaking and writing in favor of the people of the Outer Banks seceding from North Carolina and re-entering the Union on their own. On October 12, a convention of 111 delegates from Hyde County, of which Hatteras was a part, met on Hatteras Island near the inlet and adopted a resolution denouncing secession and the Confederacy and proclaiming their loyalty to the Federal government. They also called for a second convention to meet at Hatteras November 18 to establish a Unionist government and elected temporary officers.

Foster and Taylor exaggerated the level of loyalty to the United States that prevailed on the coast of North Carolina. But their claims were not without some basis in fact. Of the 250 registered voters on Hatteras Island in the presidential election of 1860, only nineteen voted for Breckinridge, the secession candidate. The rest of the vote, forty-three each, was split between Douglas and Lincoln, even though the latter was not even on the ballot. Furthermore, following the Battle of Chicamacomico, the fleeing Confederates burned a number of the Bankers' houses to prevent their use by the enemy, and they confiscated a number of local fishing boats. Such heavy-handed action by the Confederates led the locals to side with their Union occupiers. Two hundred and fifty residents of Hatteras Island took the oath of allegiance when the Federals first landed. Commander Rowan noted shortly after seizing Hatteras that "there are thousands of loyal men on the waters of the sounds who only want protection to make themselves heard and felt in this struggle." Colonel Hawkins had reported that secret Union meetings were being held in the counties bordering Pamlico Sound, and he confidently predicted that "one-third of the state of North Carolina [will] be back in the Union within two weeks." When such an uprising failed to materialize, Hawkins tempered his assessment of Union strength: "Those [coastal residents loyal to the United States] were Unionists in feeling, partly through a dislike of the war, and a desire to avoid military service for the Confederacy, and partly also by fear of the Federal forces at whose mercy they were placed on account of the lack of any coastal defenses." A number of Bankers and other coastal residents joined the two regiments of Union infantry composed of native North Carolinians known as "buffaloes." To be sure, not all Outer Bankers supported their invaders. At the same time as some were taking the oath of allegiance and joining the Federal ranks, others were crossing the sounds and enlisting in Confederate units such as the Thirty-third North Carolina Regiment being formed in Hyde County in the autumn of 1861. Spier Singleton, M.D., superintendent of the Marine Hospital on Portsmouth Island, promptly left Portsmouth when the Federals arrived and offered his much needed medical service to the Confederacy. Historian David Stick has written that "Whether the Union sentiment, especially on Hatteras Island, was of the genuine, inbred type or simply an expedient to make the best of changing conditions, the fact is that many of the Bankers did side with the North." Those who chose that course suffered as the result of the loss of their market with the mainland for the sale of fish and other seafood. They also lost the ability to trade with the mainland, and their supplies of salt, flour, and other food became short. To help alleviate the destitute condition of those on the Outer Banks who had professed loyalty to the United States, a number of prominent Northerners decided to hold a special meeting on November 7, 1861, at Cooper Institute in New York to hear about the plight of the Unionists on Hatteras Island. Among those influential persons attending were the historian and former U.S. secretary of the navy George Bancroft, the poet William Cullen Bryant, the wealthy businessmen and philanthropists John J. Astor and William E. Dodge, and General Burnside. The Reverend Mr. Taylor and Rev. T. W. Conway, a chaplain with the U.S. troops on Hatteras Island, traveled to New York to speak to the delegation about the plight of the Outer Bankers and to request supplies for their relief. Foster was also in attendance, and he seized the opportunity to harangue the gathering with the preposterous news that he had personally received authority to represent nearly thirty counties at the upcoming Hatteras convention of November 18. With typical hyperbole, Foster told the assembly that thousands of loyal North Carolinians had flocked to the U.S. colors since the landing at Hatteras. The audience expressed outrage at the conditions of the Bankers and the treatment they had received at the hands of the Confederates. They formed a "relief committee" of prominent men, raised money, and eventually dispatched the schooner E. *Sheddon* to Hatteras with supplies. By the time the vessel arrived at the inlet, however, "a profitable employment had been afforded to the natives by the soldiers, which relieved the wants of the people, so that a considerable portion of the produce sent for charity was sold and the money returned to the New York Committee." Lincoln cautiously endorsed the Cooper Institute gathering, calling it a "mission for charity" for "the relief of Union people of North Carolina." The president said of Taylor, "I have no doubt that [he is] true and faithful, and that [his] mission of charity is most worthy and praiseworthy." But Lincoln, despite his desire to support substantial and legitimate Unionism in the Confederacy, carefully avoided giving any endorsement or legitimacy to Foster and his bogus attempts to create a loyal government on the Outer Banks.

Foster and Taylor nonetheless went ahead with their plans for the convention at Hatteras on November 18, 1861. The convention listed forty-five counties as represented by delegates, but in actuality no more than eight men were present, with Taylor and Foster holding the bulk of the proxy votes. The convention declared North Carolina's articles of secession null and void and appointed Taylor provisional governor. Assuming his office, Taylor called for an election for North Carolina's Second U.S. Congressional District. On election day, voting was held at schoolhouses at Hatteras Island's four precincts in the villages of Hatteras, Chicamacomico, Kinnekeet, and Trent (later called Frisco). Of the 268 votes cast, all were unanimous in support of Taylor for governor and Foster as U.S. representative to Congress. (The pre-war Second District had over 9,000 voters.) The Federal Congress soon declined to validate Foster's election and refused him a seat in the House. Still undeterred, the rump government of Governor Taylor called for a second election on January 16, 1862.

Unfortunately for the governor and Foster, bad weather interfered with voter turnout on the sixteenth. The Burnside expedition also impeded the number of voters who ventured to the polls. However, Foster claimed victory anyway but then decided to reschedule the vote for January 30. On that occasion, he won yet again, this time receiving 298 votes. As might be expected, Congress refused to recognize this election also. Still, for a number of months, Foster persisted in his political ambition to garner the Unionist vote and ascend to the U.S. Congress. When New Bern fell to the Federals in March 1862, he convinced the commanding officer of the Twenty-fifth Massachusetts Regiment to provide a platform and military band for a political rally that he planned to hold, but Burnside forbade that activity, as the town was still under martial law. (One interesting document composed by Foster gave some hint at the circumstances surrounding his efforts to be elected to Congress. Ostensibly from citizens of Carteret County proclaiming their support of Foster, many of the signatures on the petition were of the same handwriting, although probably not that of Foster himself.)

Foster and Taylor's activities were denounced by North Carolinians loyal to the Confederacy. The bogus government at Hatteras had been organized by "the Yankees and their fish canker prisoners," cried the *North Carolina Whig* of Charlotte. The *Fayetteville Observer* remarked that the "Governor of the wreckers [Outer Bankers]" would not wish to return and face the hostility of the citizens of Robeson County, where Taylor owned land and slaves. The *Observer* declared that Foster was a "vile scoundrel," who was only interested in his own advancement and deserved to be rejected by his "Yankee brethren."

Undeterred, Foster appeared yet again before the Congressional Committee on Elections on June 5, 1862, but this time he could only make his appeal on the basis of public opinion in the coastal counties and not upon the existence of a loyal government at Hatteras. He had lost any legitimate claim as head of a de facto Unionist government because on May 19 Lincoln had appointed Edward Stanly as military governor of North Carolina with headquarters at New Bern. With the Hatteras government then without any claim to legitimacy at all, the Reverend Mr. Taylor abandoned the Outer Banks and faded into obscurity. His secretary, Alonzo Stowe, changed his loyalties, went over to the Confederate side, and eventually was captured while running the blockade at Wilmington and imprisoned at New Bern. A Federal commission called for Foster to appear and barred him from returning to North Carolina for the rest of the war.

But Foster was nothing if not persistent, and still considering himself the champion of Unionism in the Tar Heel State, he appealed to Lincoln for permission to form a U.S. regiment of North Carolinians who were loyal to the Federal government. With some reservation, Lincoln appointed him a captain and gave him authority to recruit Union sympathizers for U.S. regiments. Foster arrived back in North Carolina in August 1862. He began recruiting soldiers for the First and Second Regiments, North Carolina Union Volunteers and commanded companies in those regiments. The eastern North Carolinians who joined those two units were known by

Among the "Buffaloes," or coastal North Carolinians who joined the Federal army, was Bertie County native Cpl. Charles Freeman of Company C, First Regiment North Carolina Union Volunteers. Photograph courtesy of Delores Forehand and Gerald Thomas.

Federals and Confederates alike as "buffaloes," a term of various and indefinite origins. The soldiers whom Foster recruited were in large measure local refugees and deserters from the Confederate army. Most of them were farmers, fishermen, craftsmen, and laborers. Less than 10 percent of them owned a slave or had enough money to buy one. At least 108 men in the First North Carolina and 100 in the Second North Carolina had previously served in the Confederate army and were frequently referred to as "turncoats." The buffaloes primarily served in Federally occupied eastern North Carolina towns. They defended Plymouth, Washington, Portsmouth, New Bern, as well as Forts Clark, Hatteras, and Macon. The companies of the First and Second Regiments, unlike companies in other U.S. regiments, did not form and operate as a regimental unit. Rather they were organized individually in certain coastal counties and never completely came together, even after the two regiments were merged into one in February 1865. Because many of the buffaloes were known to have deserted from the Confederate army, Confederate general George E. Pickett ordered twenty-two prisoners from the Second Regiment North Carolina Union Volunteers hanged near Kinston as deserters following a failed attempt by Pickett to recapture New Bern in February 1864. Coastal North Carolinians who joined the Union army lived in constant fear that if forced to surrender they might be tortured and executed by their Confederate captors. As the tide of battle turned against the Federals at the Battle of Plymouth in April 1864, many of them broke and ran rather than face capture.

Following the execution of the members of the Second U.S. North Carolina Regiment at Kinston, Foster traveled to Fort Monroe, Virginia, to recruit more soldiers. While he was there, Gen. Benjamin F. Butler, then commanding the Army of the James with headquarters at Fort Monroe, appointed him a provisional lieutenant colonel. Butler's subsequent investigation, however, led him to suggest to the War Department that Foster be dropped from the army and his duties as a recruiter reassigned. That ended Foster's military career. After the war, he returned to Murfreesboro, where he became a businessman, practiced law, and wrote for various newspapers and periodicals. In 1878 he and his wife and three daughters and a son moved to Philadelphia, where he became an editorial writer for the *Philadelphia Record*. He died in Philadelphia in 1882.

Edward Stanly, the man who ultimately received Lincoln's appointment as military governor in the Tar Heel State, was a native Tar Heel. He had been born in New Bern in 1810. He attended the University of North Carolina for one term and continued his education in Connecticut. He then studied law and opened a practice in Washington, N.C. In 1837 Stanly was elected to Congress from Beaufort County as a Whig, and he served in the state House of Commons in 1844-1846. The state legislature elected him attorney general in 1847, but he resigned in the following year and returned to the House of Commons. In 1849 he again took his seat in Congress. As a confirmed Whig and a strong proponent of the Union, Stanly supported the Compromise of 1850 and other measures to avoid civil war. In the congressional elections of 1851, he campaigned against the doctrine of secession and was reelected to the U.S. House of Representatives. With the decline of the Whig Party in North Carolina in 1852, he left the state and established a law practice in San Francisco.

In 1857 Stanly ran unsuccessfully for governor of California as the candidate of the newly formed Republican Party (now the party of Lincoln, also a former Whig), although Stanly (unlike Lincoln) disagreed with that party's opposition to the extension of slavery into the territories acquired as a result of the Mexican War. As the sectional crisis intensified, he spoke out against secession and on behalf of maintaining the Union. Once the Civil War began, he offered to return to North Carolina as a peace emissary. Responding to the favorable results of the appointment of Andrew Johnson as military governor of Tennessee, Lincoln sought to establish such an official in occupied North Carolina. At the suggestion of Secretary of State William L. Seward, the president asked Stanly to take the appointment. Stanly accepted and arrived in New Bern in May 1862 in the midst of a ferocious thunderstorm. Burnside, though ill at the time, was on hand to greet the new provisional governor, and Stanly presented the general with a letter of introduction from Secretary of War Edwin M. Stanton. After pleasantries were exchanged, Stanly confided in Burnside the "painful responsibility" that he felt in the new posting. Apparently, Burnside was favorably impressed by Stanly, writing later to Stanton that he would "grant him every facility" to carry out his duties. "Indeed," writes historian William C. Harris, "Burnside agreed with Lincoln that North Carolina was ripe for reconstruction." The general reported to the president "there is much true

Edward Stanly, a New Bern native, was Abraham Lincoln's provisional governor for Federally occupied coastal North Carolina. Photograph of engraving from the State Archives.

loyalty here, and all the people are heartily sick of the war. . . . The arrival of Governor Stanley [sic] will, I hope, do a great deal of good."

But even with the support of the Union army, Stanly had a formidable task. Although the U.S. Army had occupied and secured the area around the sounds, its control did not extend far beyond its fortifications and the range of its gunboats on the rivers and sounds. Beyond the Union lines, Federal and Confederate raiding parties seeking supplies frequently preyed upon the farms and plantations of the countryside. Many inhabitants had fled the area to seek safety in the towns of the interior. Near New Bern, one Connecticut soldier remarked on "the ruin, devastation, and utter abandonment of villages, plantations, and farms, which but a short time ago were peopled, fenced, and stocked, houses once comfortable that are now either burned or deserted, barns in ashes all along the roadside, fences destroyed for miles and over thousands of acres, no cows, horses, sheep, or poultry to be seen." Thousands of poor white refugees and escaped slaves poured into New Bern and other Federally controlled sites seeking aid and protection. Such conditions further convinced Stanly that the early restoration of civil government to North Carolina and the state's return to the Union could save the inhabitants from further hardships and devastation. He did what he could to protect the residents from the plundering by raiders and to maintain law and order within his jurisdiction. At public gatherings he promoted Lincoln's plan to restore North Carolina to the Union. He assured coastal North Carolinians that Lincoln would not call for the abolition of slavery as a requirement for reunion but that the president wanted to reestablish the Union as it had been before the war. He told them that "Mr. Lincoln . . . is the best friend the South has got."

To help Lincoln carry out his plans for restoration of North Carolina to the United States, Stanly followed the president's orders to make contact with the newly elected Confederate governor of North Carolina, Zebulon B. Vance. Vance, who took office in September 1862, had also been a Unionist and Whig prior to the war and was elected governor with the support of the state's wartime Conservative Party, comprised of voters who had originally opposed secession. Stanly sought an interview with Vance to discuss the possibility of reunion for North Carolina. Vance, however, would have nothing to do with Stanly and strongly rebuffed his overture.

At Lincoln's urging, Stanly also held congressional elections in coastal North Carolina. On December 10, 1862, he called for the election to be held on January 1. The candidates were former North Carolina Whig legislator and Unionist Jennings Pigott and the never-tiring political opportunist Charles H. Foster. All white men who had lived in North Carolina for one year could vote in the election. Only three counties in the eleven-county district held the election, and a mere 864 votes were cast. Pigott won overwhelmingly. Foster received only a few votes. But the U.S. House of Representatives, having held hearings that discussed congressional elections in other occupied districts in the South, refused to accept Pigott.

By the end of 1862, Stanly had made a conscientious effort to carry out Lincoln's plan for establishing a loyal government in North Carolina. At the outset of his mission, he and Lincoln had been, for the most part, in agreement about the purpose of the war and the wisdom of bringing the state back into the Union. They both maintained that the conflict was being fought to restore the seceded Southern states to the United States and that the abolition of slavery was not a Federal objective. But during Stanly's tenure as provisional governor, Lincoln appeared to have changed his stance on slavery and the goals of the Union war effort. The president also came to realize that he had overestimated Unionist sentiment in North Carolina and would soon abandon his plans for wartime reconstruction in the state. Thus in disagreement with Lincoln's apparent change of heart regarding the mission of the war, Stanly resigned his position as military governor. Perhaps the people who played the largest role in bringing about Stanly's resignation and changing Lincoln's mind about the objectives of the war were the African Americans of North Carolina.

7 African Americans and Their Struggle for Freedom

No one had their lives changed more profoundly by the Civil War than did the millions of African Americans, mostly slaves, who inhabited the South. As early as 1790, 31 percent of North Carolina families owned slaves. At the outbreak of the conflict, North Carolina had 331,059 slaves and 30,463 free blacks. Those African Americans constituted over one-third of the state's population. Their numbers in the total population of the state grew from 29.3 percent in 1800 to 36.5 percent on the eve of the war. The number of slaves varied from a minority in the western region of North Carolina to large holdings in the Piedmont and Coastal Plain.

All the coastal counties included slaves. In 1860 enforced black laborers comprised more than 50 percent of the total populations of Bertie (over 58 percent), Chowan, and Perquimans Counties at the head of Albemarle Sound. The other coastal counties had slave populations of between 40 and 50 percent of their total populations, with the exceptions of Tyrrell, Hyde, and Carteret Counties, which had slave populations of 33, 37, and 25 percent respectively. The Outer Banks contained few slaves, primarily because the area was not suitable for farming. Only Roanoke Island produced any significant number of crops, and even that was small compared to farming on the mainland. And slavery, of course, flourished in areas of large-scale agriculture. Consequently, the owners of large plantations producing staple crops such as cotton and tobacco had the greatest numbers of slaves. Nevertheless, throughout most of North Carolina, the majority of slaveholders were small-scale farmers who owned three or fewer black laborers. In the coastal region, slaves also worked in the turpentine industry and as watermen, stevedores, sailors, pilots, and fishermen.

Like slaves, the majority of free blacks worked on farms and plantations, often alongside their enslaved brethren. But a significant number of free blacks lived in towns and followed such skilled occupations as barber, blacksmith, cabinetmaker, and carpenter. Others were peddlers, woodyard operators, or owned or worked in livery stables and hauling businesses. Both New Bern and Wilmington had sizable free black populations. A few free blacks amassed considerable property and wealth and even purchased slaves of their own.

Whether slave or free, African Americans in North Carolina lived under difficult conditions, with many restrictions. As the clash between North and South over the slavery issue continued to intensify in the prewar years, North Carolina passed laws that increasingly inhibited the lives and activities of African Americans. In 1830 the General Assembly approved a law prohibiting anyone from teaching a slave to read and write. The law also ended the practice of a master merely receiving permission from a county court to free one of his slaves. Under the new statute, masters had to post bond for aged or favored slaves. All others, upon being granted their freedom, had to leave the state within ninety days "and never thereafter return."

After the 1831 Nat Turner rebellion in Southampton County, Virginia, excited terror and panic in North Carolina, the state courts strengthened controls over slave movement and gave greater powers to slave patrols. The courts even suggested that it was permissible for a master to murder his slave under certain circumstances. In one case the North Carolina Supreme Court ruled that "the homicide of a slave may be extenuated by acts, which would not produce a legal provocation if done by a white person." In another case, the court declared that "The power of the master must be absolute to render the submission of the slave perfect." White North Carolinians' fears that their slaves might stage an insurrection were also compounded by the publication of African American David Walker's *Appeal in Four Articles*, which appeared in print in 1829. Born in Wilmington in 1785 of a free mother and a slave father, Walker, by law, took the status of his mother and was free. He migrated to Boston, where he became a clothier. His *Appeal* denounced the sin of slavery and cautioned whites that some day their slaves might rise up in bloody rebellion and extract revenge for their years in bondage. The pamphlet circulated in the cities of the South including the coastal ports of Wilmington and New Bern. The attempted slave insurrection led by the abolitionist John Brown in neighboring Virginia in 1859 further added to the terror of North Carolinians that their slaves might revolt and massacre them. Restrictions and surveillance by slave patrols and other authorities tightened as the nation moved closer to the crescendo of civil war.

Free blacks also suffered a growing loss of control over their liberties. In 1826 the General Assembly passed a law prohibiting free blacks from entering North Carolina. In 1835 legislators revoked free blacks' right to vote. Other laws passed prior to the war denied free blacks the right to preach in public, to possess firearms without a special license, to buy or sell liquor, or to attend any public school. Finally in 1861, the lawmakers prohibited any black from owning or controlling a slave. That measure prevented any free black from purchasing the freedom of his wife, child, or other relatives who were slaves.

Conditions of slavery varied from locale to locale and from master to master. But regardless of where it existed or whether a slaveholder was a kind or cruel man, slavery was a wretched institution that held little benefit or pleasure for the human beings who were held captive for their labor. Some of the best descriptions of slavery in coastal North Carolina have been related by the former slaves themselves in the slave narratives collected by the Works Progress Administration during the Great Depression. One former slave, Henry James Trentham, recalled his life on a large plantation in Camden County, bordering Albemarle Sound:

> I was born on a plantation near Camden NC. I belonged to Dr. Trentham and my missus was named Elizabeth. My father was named James Trentham, and my mother was named Lorie. I had two brothers and one sister. We all belonged to Dr. Trentham. . . . Master's plantation was an awful big plantation with about four hundred slaves on it. It was a Short distance from the Wateree River. Master lived in a large two story house with about twelve rooms in it. We called it the plantation house. Master and missus rode around in a carriage drawn by two horses and driven by a driver. They had four women to work in the house as cooks, maids, and the like. . . . The slave houses looked like a small town and there was grist mills for corn, a cotton gin, shoe shops, tanning yards, and lots of looms for weaving cloth. Most of the slaves cooked at their own houses, that they called shacks. They was given an allowance of rations every week. The rations was tolerably good, just about like people eat now. Our master looked after us when we got sick. . . . Master had four overseers on the place, and they drove us from sunup to sunset. Some of the females plowed barefooted most of the time, and had to carry that row and keep up with the men, and then do their cooking at night. We hated to see the sunrise in slavery time, 'cause it meant another hard day, but then we was glad to see it go down. . . . The corn-shuckings was a great time. Masters give good liquor to everybody then. When anybody shucked a red ear, he got an extra drink of

whiskey. We had big suppers then, and a good time at cornshuckings. After the shucking, at night, there would be wrestling match to see who was the best on the plantation. We got a week holiday at Christmas. . . . Shoes was give to the slaves, and the good times generally lasted a week. At lay-by time was another big time. That was about the fourth of July. They give a big dinner and everybody ate all the barbeque [and] cake they wanted. . . . There was a church on the plantation, and both white and black went to preaching there. There was Sunday school there too. The preacher told us to obey our missus and master. He told us we must be obedient to them. Yes sir, that's what he told us. They would not allow slaves no books, and I can't read and write. I didn't get any learning. . . . No hunting was allowed any slave if no white man was with him, and they was not allowed to carry guns. . . . There was a jail on the place to put slaves in, and in the jail there was a place to put your hands in, called stocks. Slaves was put there for punishment. I see'd lots of slaves whupped by the overseers. The pattyrollers [slave patrollers] come 'round ever now and then, and if you was off the plantation and had no pass, they tore you up with the lash. Some of the slaves run away. When they was caught, they was whupped and put in the stocks in the jail. Some of the slaves that run away never did come back. The overseers told us they got killed, reason they never come back. . . . When a slave died, there was only a few to go to the burying. They didn't have time to go, they was so busy working. The slaves was buried in plain wooden boxes which was made by slave men on the plantation. . . . I saw slaves sold at Camden. Master carried some slaves there and put them on the auction block and sold them. I was carried, but I was not sold. I went with the old doctor. I was his pet. They carried slaves away from the plantation in chains. They carried five or six at a time. If a nigger didn't suit him, he sold him. Missus didn't like for him to beat them so much no how.

The ninety-six-year-old former slave Samuel Riddick recounted his experience on a plantation in Perquimans County near Albemarle Sound:

I was born the fourth day of February 1841. My owners, my white people, my old mistress wrote me a letter telling me my age. My mother was Nancy Riddick. She belonged to the Riddicks in the eastern part of the state. My father was named Elisha Riddick. My master was Elisha, and my mistress Sara Riddick. I was born in Perquimans County, NC, and I have lived in North Carolina all my life. We had good food for master was a heavy farmer. There were about 200 acres cleared on the plantation, and about 25 slaves. The great house was where master lived, and the quarters was where we lived. They were near the great house. I saw only one slave whupped. I had mighty fine white people, yes, might fine. They did not whup their slaves, but their son whupped my mother pretty bad, because she did not bale enough corn and turnips to feed the fattening hogs. . . . [The son] was a rangtang. He loved his liquor and he loved colored women. The old man never whupped anybody. I have seen pattyrollers. They were my friends. I had friends among them. Because I had a young missus they run with. That's why they let me alone. I went with her to cotton pickings at night. They came, but they didn't touch me. My young missus married Dr. Perry from the same neighborhood in Perquimans County. . . . There were no half-white children on master's plantation and no mixups that ever came out to be disgrace in anyway. My white folks was fine people. I remember master's brother's son Tommy going off to the war. Master's brother was named Willis Riddick. He never came back. When the war broke out I left my master and went to Portsmouth, VA. [Union] General [Nelson A.] Miles captured me and put me in uniform. I waited on him as a body servant, a private in the U.S. Army. I stayed with him until General Lee surrendered. . . . I haven't anything to say against slavery. My old folks put clothes on me when I was a boy. They gave me shoes and stockings and put them on me when I was a little boy. I loved them, and I can't go against them in anything. There were things I did not like about slavery on some plantations, whuppings and selling parents and childrens from each other, but I haven't much to say. I was treated good.

With the arrival of Burnside's expedition on Roanoke Island in February 1862, slaves throughout coastal North Carolina heard rumors that Yankee soldiers had invaded the state and were liberating blacks from bondage. Hundreds, eventually thousands, of slaves acted on that news and seized the opportunity to flee their masters and seek refuge and freedom under the protection of Federal guns. Although the Emancipation Proclamation was still months in the future, the U.S. Army had already begun treating escaped slaves as freedmen. At Fort Monroe, Virginia, in 1861 Gen. Benjamin F. Butler had established the precedent of protecting runaway slaves. He designated blacks who fled to his lines as "contraband of war" and refused to return them to their masters. He used them as laborers for his army and assigned them the name of "contrabands," which for a time applied to both slaves captured by the Union army and as a slang word for African Americans in general.

By the late spring of 1862, the number of escaped slaves on Roanoke Island had grown to about one thousand. Most of these had been put to work by the Federals. "Contraband" pay on the island was ten dollars per month for men, plus food and clothing, and four dollars per month, plus food and clothing, for women. Teenage boys received four dollars per month and rations. Children under thirteen received food. Burnside's officers put the escaped slaves to work building new docks and a wharf and

When U.S. troops seized coastal North Carolina, thousands of African American slaves fled their masters and found refuge within Union lines. Shown here are former slaves gathered in front of the provost marshal's office in New Bern. Photograph by O. J. Smith reproduced courtesy of the North Carolina Collection, University of North Carolina Library, Chapel Hill.

Massachusetts soldier Champney made this and the following three drawings of some of the black refugees who sought freedom within Union lines. From the Outer Banks History Center.

storage facilities, shoring up batteries, and repairing damaged forts and earthworks. The "contrabands" unloaded and loaded the steady stream of steamers needed to support further military operations on the sounds.

When New Bern fell to Federal attack in March 1862 and slaves learned that their Union liberators had captured the city, large numbers of them stole away from their masters and traveled to the occupied area seeking freedom. They left the farms and plantations, hid in the swamps or woods at night, and then made their way usually to New Bern but also to Washington, Elizabeth City, Plymouth, Beaufort, or other places held by the Union army. Hattie Rogers, an Onslow County slave, described the flight of some African Americans to escape bondage: "When the Yankees took New Bern, all who could swim the [White Oak] River and get to the Yankees were free. Some of the men swum the river and got to Jones County then to New Bern and freedom." Many of the blacks who took flight were like George Harris of Jones County. He recounted his escape: "We lived near Trenton. When de Yankees took New Bern, our master had us out in de woods in Jones County mindin hosses an' taking care o' things he had hid there. We got afraid and ran away to New Bern in Craven County. We all went in a gang and walked. De Yankees took us at Deep Gully ten miles dis side o' New Bern an' carried us inside de lines." When the Federals raided into the interior—Goldsboro, Kinston, or Tarboro—many slaves joined them on their return march to New Bern. "Every expedition to the interior . . . was a sign for great numbers to come in," recalled Cpl. James A. Emmerton of the Twenty-third Massachusetts Regiment. "There is perhaps not a slave in North Carolina who does not know he can find freedom in New Bern, and thus New Bern may be Mecca of a thousand noble aspirations."

As on Roanoke Island, the Federals utilized the skills, knowledge, and labor of the fugitive slaves. The "contrabands" built fortifications at various sites, including Fort Totten at New Bern. They unloaded about three hundred steamers at that port and became permanent labor gangs for the quartermaster and ordnance offices. They constructed a large railroad bridge across the Trent River to replace the one burned by the Confederates during the battle of New Bern in March 1862. At New Bern black laborers were paid $10 per month. Stevedores in New Bern earned $15 per month and teamsters $20. Wages for carpenters, blacksmiths, masons, and mechanics ranged from $1.25 to $3.00 per day. At New Bern, more than fifteen hundred African Americans were employed by November 1863. About fifty escaped slaves served as spies, scouts, and guides for the Union army.

The Confederate government, too, used North Carolina slaves, on temporary loan from their owners, to work on fortifications, particularly at Fort Fisher. But most slaveholders resented this impressment of their labor force and constantly complained that Confederate officers were keeping their slaves too long when they were needed back home to work in the fields, especially at harvest time. At times, slaves working on Confederate defenses seized the opportunity of being away from their masters to escape and take refuge within Federal protection.

Officials in Washington, D.C., added their support to the actions of U.S. Army officers in the field to guarantee the liberty of "contrabands." In June 1862, President Abraham Lincoln reportedly proclaimed that "no slave who once comes within our lines as a fugitive from a rebel, shall ever be returned to his master." In July, Congress passed a confiscation act declaring that slaves who took refuge behind Union lines were captives of war who were to be set free. Those edicts did not, however, apply to those slave owners who were still loyal to the Union. It would be the Emancipation Proclamation, first issued as a preliminary document in September 1862 and then in its final form in January 1863, finally to liberate all slaves within

Champney drawing from the Outer Banks History Center.

Champney drawing from the Outer Banks History Center.

Champney drawing from the Outer Banks History Center.

states then in rebellion against the United States. (Ratified in 1865, the Thirteenth Amendment to the United States Constitution would ensure that the prohibition of slavery throughout the nation would have a permanent basis in Federal law.)

Day by day, the influx of African Americans fleeing from bondage continued to grow within Union lines in coastal North Carolina. In October 1862 a Beaufort County slaveholder noted that "It is nothing uncommon for dozens of slaves to escape from one man in a day, or for a plantation to be effectually ruined in a few hours." In August 1862, one Confederate official estimated the monetary value of escaped slaves to be $1 million per week. Even if that figure might have been an exaggeration, the loss of revenue, nevertheless, was substantial when one considers that a young male field hand was worth as much as $1,000. Furthermore, the flight of thousands of slaves represented a considerable drop in the state's labor force and a corresponding decline in income in a labor intensive agricultural economy.

To cope with the swelling population of African Americans and to deal also with many white refugees seeking aid, General Burnside appointed Vincent Colyer as superintendent of the poor for Federally occupied North Carolina. A former agent for the New York YMCA, Colyer had already worked with the "contrabands" on Roanoke Island before establishing his

As "contrabands," many escaped slaves found employment with the Union army as laborers, teamsters, and skilled artisans. These African Americans are water carriers for the army on Hatteras Island. Champney drawing from the Outer Banks History Center.

headquarters at New Bern. In addition to supplying provisions to escaped slaves and destitute whites, Colyer had his charges vaccinated for smallpox and persuaded Burnside to establish a government hospital for blacks. He also organized African American churches and began a number of schools for blacks and poor whites in New Bern. He employed a young female resident to teach in the white school. The blacks had two evening schools with a total of eight hundred pupils, young and old. A number of the soldiers of the New England regiments, some of whom were college graduates, volunteered as teachers.

Colyer's efforts to educate the African Americans whose welfare had been entrusted to him met with strong opposition from provisional governor Edward Stanly. Stanly was not particularly sympathetic to the plight of the freed slaves in eastern North Carolina. In fact, as mentioned previously, he had accepted Lincoln's appointment as governor because he believed that Lincoln would not insist on emancipation as a goal of the Federal war effort. Although Stanly approved Colyer's efforts to feed and clothe contrabands as well as white refugees, he strongly opposed educating blacks and ordered the superintendent of the poor to close his evening schools. He also attempted to return a female slave to her owner, and that action enraged many of the New England troops in New Bern in addition to many antislavery advocates in the North. The provisional governor maintained that he "had been sent to restore the old order of things," which meant that he would enforce North Carolina's old antebellum laws regarding blacks.

An African American laborer at an army cookhouse in Federally occupied New Bern. Champney drawing from the Outer Banks History Center.

Alarmed by Stanly's behavior, Colyer traveled to Washington, D.C., and talked with Radical Republicans and abolitionists like Senator Charles Sumner of Massachusetts. He also met with President Lincoln who assured him that he had not given Stanly instructions to enforce prewar North Carolina laws, nor had he approved the return of fugitive slaves to their masters. Colyer then returned to New Bern, where he began a conciliatory cooperation with Stanly in exchange for the governor reopening the evening schools for blacks. To many of the New England troops, it appeared that Colyer, to placate Stanly, was going to devote more attention to white refugees than to needy African Americans, and they became disillusioned with him. Partly because of that disillusionment, Colyer departed New Bern with Burnside when the general was transferred to the Army of the Potomac in the summer of 1862. Burnside's successor, Gen. John G. Foster, appointed army chaplain the Reverend James Means to replace Colyer as superintendent of the poor.

Stanly was not long in following Colyer in departing New Bern. The issuance of the Emancipation Proclamation in January 1863 was a measure that Stanly would not accept, and he resigned his position as U.S. military or provisional governor of North Carolina. His understanding of his mission had been that he was to bring the state back into the Union with the antebellum status quo still in effect, including the institution of slavery. He believed that the sectional conflict was "a war of restoration and not of abolition and destruction." Furthermore, his efforts to engender or renew loyalty to the Union in eastern North Carolina had met with little success. Stanly's failure also demonstrated to Lincoln that he had overestimated the strength of Unionism in North Carolina, and he thereafter abandoned his plans to bring the state back into the Union with a loyal government during the war.

Not only did the Emancipation Proclamation offer the slaves of the Confederacy the promise of freedom, it gave escaped slaves in coastal

Among the free blacks who lived in coastal North Carolina was Mary Jane Conner, who ran a boardinghouse in New Bern. Tintype (June 1863) from the collection of Tryon Palace Historic Sites & Gardens, New Bern.

North Carolina the opportunity to fight for the liberation of their relatives and friends still in bondage. The proclamation provided for the official recruitment of African Americans into the U.S. Army, and soon after its issuance, recruitment of blacks into Federal ranks began in earnest in coastal North Carolina. In April 1863, the U.S. War Department authorized Col. Edward A. Wild of Boston to organize a brigade of black troops in the Department of North Carolina. The unit became known as the "African Brigade," and it consisted of three regiments of blacks from North Carolina and one regiment, the Fifty-fifth Massachusetts, of Northern blacks. The North Carolina regiments were the First, Second, and Third Regiments North Carolina Colored Volunteers (later renamed the Thirty-fifth, Thirty-sixth, and Thirty-seventh Regiments United States Colored Troops). White officers commanded the brigade. A fourth infantry regiment composed of North Carolina slaves for the brigade never formed. Instead the First Regiment North Carolina Heavy Artillery (African Descent) began mustering its first company in New Bern in March 1864. Its last company was mustered in April 1865, by which time it had been renamed the Fourteenth Regiment United States Colored Heavy Artillery.

Promoted to brigadier general, Wild established his headquarters and main recruiting office in New Bern, and former slaves responded immediately to his efforts to recruit them into the African Brigade. The new recruits drilled, responded well to discipline, accepted responsibility, and acquired a soldierly quality that impressed many of the white troops. A black soldier's pay was ten dollars per month, the same as a laborer's. Former slaves who enlisted exhibited a special courage, because upon hearing of the Federal plans to recruit African Americans, Confederates vowed to treat captured black troops as insurrectionists, not prisoners of war. Later in some battles such as that at Plymouth in April 1864, Confederate soldiers summarily executed and massacred black soldiers

Following the Emancipation Proclamation issued in January 1863, the U.S. War Department enlisted African Americans into the Union army. A large number of black North Carolinians served in the African Brigade, formed in the Federally occupied coastal region. Among them was William Henry Singleton, a former Craven County slave. Singleton served throughout the war and then moved north. He is pictured here at a 1937 Grand Army of the Republic reunion in Gettysburg, Pennsylvania. Photograph courtesy of Laurel Vlock, New Haven, Connecticut.

who surrendered or were captured.

On July 30, 1863, Wild and the troops of the African Brigade embarked for South Carolina. As they left New Bern, they proudly carried a banner that had been presented to them by the Colored Ladies Union Relief Association, which had paid for the flag from funds collected "from their own people." The troops departed North Carolina in such haste that they left behind much of their equipment. In South Carolina the brigade took part in Gen. Quincy A. Gillmore's unsuccessful attempt to capture Fort Wagner, the key defense to Charleston harbor. Wild's men spent most of their time on Folly Island and saw little action.

But after returning with his brigade to North Carolina in October 1863, Wild received orders from Gen. Benjamin F. Butler, commanding the Department of Virginia and North Carolina (which then included the old Department of North Carolina), to travel to Norfolk with two of his regiments. On December 5, Butler ordered Wild and his two regiments into the northeastern area of North Carolina. The purpose of the expedition was to reopen navigation on the Dismal Swamp Canal, to protect Unionists from Confederate guerrillas, and to lure away slaves from their masters and enlist as many as possible into the Union army. During their

Troops of the African Brigade, led by white colonel Edward A. Wild, are shown here liberating slaves in northeastern North Carolina. Engraving from *Harper's Weekly*, 1864.

raid, Wild's troops liberated twenty-five hundred slaves, burned four guerrilla camps, and captured fifty guns and much ammunition, supplies, and equipment. They took several prisoners, hanged one guerrilla, and captured many horses, as well as four large boats hauling war contraband. According to historian John G. Barrett, the raid was important because it was the first "of any magnitude undertaken [solely] by negro troops since their enlistment was authorized by Congress."

Among the troops of the African Brigade was Outer Banker Richard Etheridge, who was on Roanoke Island when the Federal army began recruiting blacks. In September 1863, Etheridge enlisted in the Second Regiment North Carolina Colored Volunteers (later the Thirty-sixth Regiment United States Colored Troops). He quickly rose to the rank of sergeant, helped with recruitment of former slaves, and served with his regiment in the Virginia campaigns. After the war, as regimental commissary sergeant, he was discharged from the army at Brazo, Texas. In July 1866, he returned to Roanoke Island and became a fisherman. In 1877 he joined the United States Lifesaving Service (a forerunner of the present-day Coast Guard) and eventually commanded the Pea Island Lifesaving Station, the only all-black station in the United States. He compiled a heroic record as lifesaver and was awarded posthumously the Gold Lifesaving Medal.

William Henry Singleton, a Craven County slave, was also a member of the African Brigade. When New Bern fell to Burnside's forces in March 1862, Singleton fled to New Bern. There he organized a drilling squad of other escaped slaves in preparation for their eventual entry into the Union army. In May 1863, he enlisted as a sergeant in Company G, First Regiment North Carolina Colored Volunteers (later the Thirty-fifth Regiment United States Colored Troops). On February 20, 1864, he was wounded at the Battle of Olustee in Florida. In November he traveled with his regiment to Hilton Head, South Carolina, and fought in the Battle of Honey Hill, near Grahamville, South Carolina. The regiment then returned to Florida and in March 1865 moved to Charleston, South Carolina, where Singleton was discharged on June 1, 1866. Singleton then moved to the North, where he lived in New England, New York, and Iowa. In 1922, he published his *Recollections of My Slavery Days*, which included accounts of his service in the U.S. Army. A much respected citizen, he was an active member of the Union veterans' organization of the Grand Army of the Republic. He died while marching in a G.A.R. parade in Des Moines, Iowa, on September 7, 1938, and was buried in New Haven, Connecticut.

By early 1864 the three North Carolina regiments of the African Brigade had ceased to exist as a distinct brigade and had been absorbed into "larger units of African American troops." As part of those larger units, however, the former slaves of coastal North Carolina would continue to serve in various locales, including Florida, North Carolina, and Virginia. Those in the Thirty-seventh Regiment United States Colored Troops (formerly the Third Regiment North Carolina Colored Volunteers) would be at the tremendous battle for Fort Fisher in February 1865. If President Lincoln ever had any doubts about the wisdom or the justness of the Emancipation Proclamation, the heroic service of black troops, such as those in the African Brigade, dispelled any reservations he might have possessed. Lincoln declared that because former slaves had taken up arms in a noble cause and demonstrated their courage and manhood as U.S. soldiers they could never be returned to slavery under any circumstances.

As many of coastal North Carolina's African American men served in the Union army, their families found refuge and shelter in the black refugee camps on the coast. The largest of those villages were the Roanoke Island Colony and the Trent River Settlement near New Bern. Most of the work and responsibility for establishing and running these camps fell to the Reverend Horace James, a chaplain from Massachusetts. More than Colyer or Means, who dealt as much with destitute whites as with blacks, James would have a great and lasting impact on African Americans in coastal North Carolina during the war.

Not long after the Reverend James Means replaced Vincent Colyer as superintendent of the poor for occupied North Carolina, Means died of yellow fever in New Bern. General Foster then searched among his officers for a replacement to deal with the thousands of fugitive slaves whose numbers were growing daily. The man he chose was Horace James, who already had considerable experience working with black refugees.

Prior to the war, James had been pastor of Old South Congregational Church in Worcester, Massachusetts. At the outbreak of the conflict, he joined the Twenty-fifth Regiment Massachusetts Infantry as a chaplain. Along with his regiment, he served under Gen. Benjamin F. Butler at Fort Monroe, where he first acquired experience working with refugee slaves. His regiment was part of the expedition that invaded Roanoke Island in

1862, and Burnside placed him in charge of the "contrabands" who flocked to the Union lines. James accompanied his regiment when it participated in the Battle of New Bern in March 1862, and after the city was secured, he immediately opened evening schools for blacks. He also provided religious instruction and obtained food and clothing from Northern philanthropic organizations, largely on his own initiative. Foster appointed James as superintendent of negro affairs, which superseded the old title of superintendent of the poor. Such offices were the forerunners of the Bureau of Refugees, Freedmen, and Abandoned Lands (the so-called Freedmen's Bureau), established by the U.S. government in March 1865. Like his predecessors, James took censuses of the escaped slaves who came under his care. He issued them rations and clothing, and he also supervised the making of contracts between former slaves and whites to ensure that those agreements were carried out by both parties.

To accommodate the ever-increasing numbers of black refugees, James and the military authorities decided to create freedmen's camps or settle-

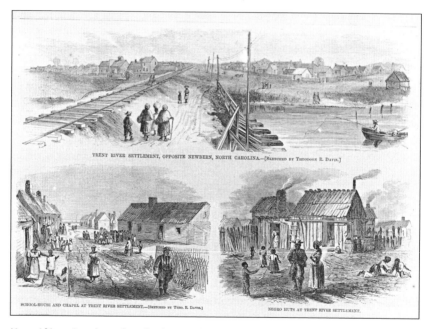

Many African Americans found refuge in the black refugee camps established by the Federals. The largest of these villages were the Roanoke Island Colony and the Trent River Settlement at New Bern. Pictured here is the Trent River Settlement. Engraving from *Harper's Weekly*, 1866.

CHAPTER SEVEN

ments on land that had been abandoned by its Confederate owners or was otherwise in Federal possession. At those sites, James planned to provide food and shelter for African American families until they could gain self-sufficiency by the means of certain programs that he intended to establish. Those programs would include basic education, vocational education, and small industries that used black workers.

James established the first of his freedmen's camps on Roanoke Island, which he hoped would serve as a model for the other settlements. He traveled north and raised $9,000 with which to purchase supplies and equipment, and he employed several teachers for his black students. He had land cleared on the island and assigned plots to black families. He also secured a sawmill, and the former slaves utilized it to build their houses and several schools. Under his supervision, some of them learned trades such as spinning, weaving, barrel making, shoemaking, shingle splitting, and fishing. Others, of course, worked for the army in various capacities, and when the African Brigade was formed, many served in its ranks. In January 1864, about 2,712 former slaves were residing on Roanoke Island. A year later, 3,091 were encamped there.

When James arrived in New Bern, he set about establishing camps there also. Originally he established three settlements in the New Bern area. But when Confederates under Maj. Gen. George Pickett attacked New Bern in 1864, two of the camps that were outside the Union fortifications had to be abandoned. As a result, Maj. Gen. John J. Peck, who had replaced General Foster as commander of the District (formerly Department) of North Carolina in August 1863, ordered James to consolidate the freedmen into one large settlement located inside the Federal perimeter and at the con-fluence of the Neuse and Trent Rivers. "It was immediately done," James later wrote. "Streets were run out, and lots assigned, fifty feet by sixty feet, allowing a little garden spot to each house." The Trent River Settlement, as the camp came to be called, originally covered about thirty acres and had about 800 houses, most of which were cabins built of "shakes," short boards about four or five feet in length and split by hand. In January 1864, the settlement had 2,798 inhabitants. That number swelled to over 3,000 in the last months of the war, when the Union army of Gen. William T. Sherman invaded the state, bringing with him thousands of escaped slaves from Georgia and South Carolina. Before the war ended, the Trent River Settlement was renamed James City to honor its founder. (Today an African American community named James City still exists only a short distance south of the original freedmen's camp.) Besides the large settlements at Roanoke Island and New Bern, the Federals also had temporary freedmen's camps at various sites on the coast, including Beaufort, Plymouth, and Washington.

A census compiled by Horace James in January 1865 indicated that 17,307 African Americans were then under the protection of the Federal army in coastal North Carolina. Of that number, 10,782 were located at New Bern and vicinity. Beaufort and vicinity had 3,245. Roanoke Island and vicinity claimed 3,091, and Hatteras Island had 95. Plymouth and vicinity included 94.

At the end of the Civil War, thousands of African Americans such as those congregated in coastal North Carolina had endured a long and arduous journey out of the bonds of slavery. At the first sign that liberty might be possible, they had taken their fate into their own hands and fled to freedom. The loss of their labor had seriously injured the Confederacy's capacity to wage war. Former slaves served the Federal war effort with dedication and purpose in a variety of ways and occupations. As U.S. soldiers, they shed their blood in battle and gave their lives to liberate themselves and their loved ones. It was the sacrifice and nobility of their struggle that ultimately convinced Abraham Lincoln and many other white Americans that slavery in the United States would have to be banished completely and forever.

CHAPTER SEVEN

8 The Confederates Strike Back

Following his spectacular victory at the Battle of Fredericksburg in December 1862, Gen. Robert E. Lee dispatched one of his generals, James Longstreet, and two divisions to the south. Longstreet's mission was to protect the supply lines in coastal North Carolina and to gather provisions from that region. In order for supply routes to remain open through the rich corn country, especially east of the Chowan River, the Confederates had to keep the Federals confined to their bases in tidewater Virginia and coastal North Carolina. Since February 1863, Longstreet—one of Lee's valued corps commanders—had been in command of the Department of North Carolina and Southern Virginia. Longstreet's subordinate in North Carolina was Gen. Daniel H. Hill. In an effort to carry out Lee's orders, Longstreet moved against Suffolk, Virginia, while Hill planned attacks on New Bern and Washington in North Carolina.

Hill's tactics for operations against New Bern required a three-pronged attack on the city. The attack would be launched from Kinston. Gen. Junius Daniel and his brigade would move against New Bern by the lower Trent Road, while Gen. Beverly H. Robertson's cavalry at Kinston would move along the upper Trent Road and break up the tracks of the Atlantic and North Carolina Railroad. The brigade of Gen. James J. Pettigrew, with artillery under Maj. John C. Haskell, would approach New Bern near Barrington's Ferry and shell the Federals' Fort Anderson and gunboats on the Neuse River.

Hill launched his assault on New Bern on March 13, 1863, when Daniel captured the enemy's first line of works at Deep Gully about eight miles from New Bern. The Confederates successfully repelled a Union attempt to recapture the works. But Robertson's and Pettigrew's failures to achieve their objectives led Hill to withdraw his forces from New Bern and turn his attention toward Washington on the Pamlico-Tar River.

When Gen. John G. Foster learned that the Confederates planned to attack Washington, he immediately left New Bern for the river town, arriving just before Hill's troops. Foster discovered that Washington was garrisoned by approximately 1,200 men drawn from the Forty-fourth Massachusetts Regiment, the First North Carolina Union Volunteers

(Buffaloes), the Third New York Cavalry, and the Third New York Artillery. Those troops were supported by the gunboats *Commodore Hull*, *Ceres*, and *Louisiana*. Foster gave orders for the strengthening of fortifications and the creation of a field of fire in open terrain.

By March 30, 1863, Hill had Washington under siege. The ensuing action consisted mostly of an exchange of artillery fire. While that duel was going on, Hill's troops gathered large quantities of bacon and corn in the countryside. Foster, in the meantime, was worried about his position and sent orders to New Bern for a relief column. Gen. Henry Prince commanded the first relief expedition, which, aboard a steamer, approached the head of the Pamlico River, glimpsed Hill's fortifications, and immediately returned to New Bern. The second relief column, commanded by Gen. Francis B. Spinola, moved overland toward Washington. At Blount's Creek on April 9, Pettigrew's troops forced the Federals to retreat back to New Bern. Finally on April 13, the U.S. gunboat *Escort*, transporting the Fifth Rhode Island Regiment, ran past the Confederate batteries. Foster placed the Rhode Island soldiers in his line of works, and then on the morning of the fifteenth was aboard the *Escort* when it ran past the rebel batteries for the second time, to return to New Bern. Seeing that the Federals could reinforce and supply Washington by way of the Pamlico River, Hill began withdrawing his troops. The siege of Washington did little to enhance Hill's reputation, and many of his men considered the operation a complete failure. At best, many felt, it had been a poor use of troops and equipment. On the fifteenth, General Longstreet wrote to Hill: "We cannot afford to keep the large force that you have watching the garrison at Washington."

In late May, General Lee began withdrawing Hill's troops from North Carolina. Following his brilliant victory at the Battle of Chancellorsville, May 1-4, 1863, Lee planned an offensive across the Potomac River into Union territory, and he needed Hill's men. Foster used that opportunity to raid the interior again. In mid-May, he ordered an attack along the Atlantic and North Carolina Railroad. U.S. troops, commanded by Colonels J. Richter Jones and George H. Pierson, attacked Hill's soldiers at a Confederate outpost at Gum Swamp near Kinston. At first, the Federals carried the field, but Confederate reinforcements eventually drove them back to New Bern. After being repulsed at Gum Swamp, Federal troops in coastal North Carolina saw little fighting during the month of June.

In mid-July, Gen. Edward E. Potter, Foster's chief of staff, led cavalry raids on Greenville, Tarboro, and Rocky Mount. Those forays—in which

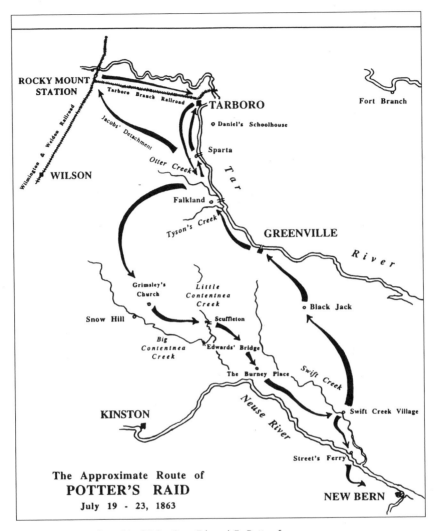

This map shows the raid of Brig. Gen. Edward E. Potter from
New Bern to Greenville, Tarboro, and Rocky Mount in July 1863.
Courtesy of David A. Norris.

supplies and property were destroyed, communications cut, and many
Confederate prisoners and "contrabands" were captured—created alarm
among many residents of eastern North Carolina, who pleaded with
Governor Vance for protection. In late July, Foster led a raid to sever the
Wilmington and Weldon Railroad at the bridge near Weldon. The raid was
foiled, however, when the Confederate brigade of Gen. Matt Ransom

repulsed the Federals at Boone's Mill and thereby prevented the destruction of the bridge. Following Boone's Mill, combat, except for minor skirmishing, ended in eastern North Carolina for the year 1863. On July 1, General Hill had relinquished command of the Department of North Carolina (a division of the Department of North Carolina and Southern Virginia) to Gen. William H. C. Whiting, commanding from Wilmington. Hill returned to the Army of Northern Virginia. July 1863 also had witnessed the devastating Confederate defeats at the Battles of Vicksburg and Gettysburg. For the rest of 1863, the Confederate war effort in the eastern theater was concentrated on Lee's army in Virginia. Relative quiet settled over the coastal counties of the Tar Heel State.

On January 2, 1864, General Lee, whose army was in winter quarters, wrote to President Jefferson Davis: "The time is at hand when, if an attempt can be made to capture the enemy's forces at New Berne, it should be done. I can now spare the troops for the purpose, which will not be the case as spring approaches. . . . A large number of provisions and other supplies are said to be at New Berne, which are much wanted for this army, besides much that is reported in the country will thus be made accessible to us." Davis agreed with Lee that the time was right to assault New Bern, and he suggested that Lee himself take charge of that initiative. Reluctant to leave his army in Virginia, Lee suggested that the New Bern expedition be commanded by Gen. Robert F. Hoke, a native Tar Heel. Hoke, however, was only a brigadier and Davis selected instead Maj. Gen. George E. Pickett, commander of the fatal and immortal charge at the Battle of Gettysburg. Davis selected his own aide, Comdr. John T. Wood, to command the cooperating naval flotilla.

The Confederates concentrated a force of approximately thirteen thousand men and fourteen naval gunboats cutters at Kinston. Pickett and his officers planned for a simultaneous assault by three Confederate columns to take place on February 1. The night before that land attack began, Commander Wood's vessels were to descend the Neuse River, capture the Federal gunboats in the river, and then cooperate with land forces in attacking New Bern. On the day of the assault, a brigade commanded by Gen. James G. Martin, dispatched by Gen. Whiting at Wilmington, was to threaten the Morehead City area in order to "fix the attention of the enemy" at that location.

Pickett divided his forces at Kinston into three columns, and on January 30 they began moving toward New Bern. Gen. Seth M. Barton commanded

In February 1864, Confederate general George E. Pickett led an unsuccessful assault to recapture New Bern. Photograph from the State Archives.

one column, which consisted of his own brigade and that of Gen. J. L. Kemper, and three regiments of Gen. Matt Ransom's brigade. Barton's mission was to cross the Trent River and continue on its south side to Brice's Creek below New Bern. After crossing the creek, he was to capture the forts along the Neuse and Trent Rivers and enter New Bern by way of the railroad bridge. Such a move would prevent the Federals from reinforcing the town from Morehead City or Beaufort. A second column commanded by Col. James Dearing, consisting of one North Carolina and two Virginia regiments, as well as artillery and three hundred cavalry, was to move along the Neuse River and capture Fort Anderson at Barrington's Ferry. General Hoke and the remaining Confederate troops were to move down the Trent and Neuse Rivers, surprise the Federal troops at Batchelder's Creek, and "silence the guns in the star fort and batteries near the Neuse, and penetrate the town in that direction." All three columns would assault New Bern simultaneously on the morning of February 1.

The attack failed. In carrying out his assignment on February 1, Hoke silenced the Federal outpost at Batchelder's Creek. He crossed the stream and then halted about a mile from New Bern, where he waited in vain to hear Barton's guns signifying that Barton's column had achieved its objective on the opposite bank of the Trent. Not until February 2 did Barton finally send word that the works on that side of the river "were too strong to attack and that he had made no advances and did not intend to." Dearing also reported that the fortifications at Fort Anderson were too formidable and he would not attack. Seeing that two of his columns had failed in their missions, Pickett withdrew his troops from New Bern.

In the meantime, however, Commander Wood and General Martin enjoyed some success in their operations. Wood and his hand-picked crew slipped down the Neuse River and on the night of February 1 boarded the U.S. steamer *Underwriter* anchored near New Bern. Wood's men fought hand to hand with the *Underwriter* crew and took possession of the vessel. The lack of enough steam to get the Federal ship under way and the harassing gunfire from a nearby fortification led Commander Wood to burn his prize and retire upriver. With similar initiative, General Martin accomplished the main objective of his assignment to focus Federal attention on Morehead City and its environs. He overran a Federal force at Newport Barracks near Morehead City and captured a vast quantity of supplies. In addition, he reported that his expedition destroyed three railroad bridges and captured four heavy dirt forts, three blockhouses, and eighty prisoners.

Following his failure to recapture New Bern, General Pickett returned to Lee's army in Virginia. General Hoke then took command of the Confederate expedition to recover territory in coastal North Carolina. Hoke abandoned for the time being attempts to take New Bern and instead turned his attention to the town of Plymouth at the mouth of the Roanoke River. Plymouth had been an important supply center for the Union army

Plymouth, on the Roanoke River, was an important supply center for the Union army. Engraving of the town in 1864 from Benson J. Lossing, *Pictorial History of the Civil War in the United States* (Philadelphia: G. W. Childs, 1868), 3:470.

throughout the war. Its commander was Gen. Henry W. Wessells, and its garrison of 2,834 men was comprised of four infantry regiments, two companies of the Second Regiment North Carolina Union Volunteers (known as "Buffaloes"), a cavalry unit, six artillery pieces for the Twenty-fourth Independent Battery New York Light Artillery, and two companies from the Second Regiment Massachusetts Heavy Artillery. Also present in Plymouth were about eighty black recruits awaiting assignment to their regiments and 1,000 "contrabands," including women and children. The citadel was protected by a ring of forts on the land side of the town. Redoubts, breastworks, and strong obstructions connected the forts. A small earthwork

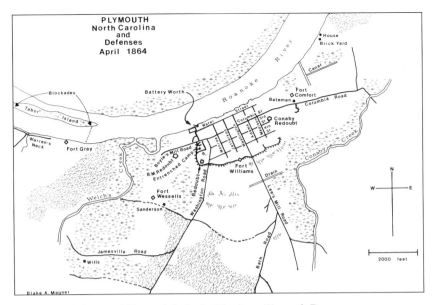

Map of the defenses of Plymouth in April 1864. From Weymoth T. Jordan Jr., comp., *North Carolina Troops, 1861–1865: A Roster.* (Raleigh: Division of Archives and History, Department of Cultural Resources, 1993), 12:564.

named Battery Worth stood on the west side of Plymouth. A line of breast-works ran south of Battery Worth to the town's southwest corner. Connected to the river on the north, this line surrounded Plymouth on all sides except the east. The open terrain to the east was guarded by several forts and redoubts as well as low, marshy ground. Also guarding the town were the gunboats *Miami* and *Southfield* and two smaller vessels, the *Whitehead* and *Ceres.* Commander C. W. Flusser commanded that flotilla, which had aboard 410 naval personnel.

To capture such a strongly fortified position as Plymouth, Hoke was con-vinced he would need naval support. Fortunately for him, the Confederates had the ironclad ram *Albemarle* under construction at Edwards Ferry on the Roanoke River. Although the construction of the vessel had been slow and hindered by many problems, including a shortage of iron, the *Albemarle* was fit for action by the time Hoke put his army into motion against Plymouth on April 17, 1864. Knowing that the ram would soon arrive to aid his assault, Hoke invested Plymouth from the land side and soon took Fort Wessells. The *Albemarle,* commanded by Comdr. James W. Cooke, arrived on the nineteenth and proceeded to attack the Federal gunboats. In prepa-

ration for the attack, the *Southfield* and the *Miami* were lashed together in the hopes of catching the Confederate ram in between them and bombarding and sinking her. But the two Union vessels became tangled in their lashings. In the heated fighting, the *Albemarle* rammed and sank the *Southfield* and drove the *Miami* downstream. Aboard the *Miami*, Commander Flusser was killed and replaced by Lt. Charles A. French. Sayres Nichols, a surgeon's steward on the *Miami*, recalled his vessel's clash with the *Albemarle*:

A Confederate attack commanded by North Carolina's Gen. Robert F. Hoke recaptured Plymouth in late April 1864. Photograph of engraving of Hoke from the State Archives.

At two in the morning, we were called to general quarters, and at three the ram jammed between us and the *Southfield*, staving her in and she sunk immediately. Part of her officers and crew reached us in safety, the rest were killed or taken prisoners. We fired thirty shells at the ram, but they had no effect on her. . . . Dr. Mann and

THE "ALBEMARLE" READY FOR ACTION.

The recapture of Plymouth made it possible for the town to serve as a port for the ironclad *Albemarle* to drive the U.S. gunboats from Albemarle and Pamlico Sounds. This engraving of the *Albemarle* is from *Century Magazine*, July 1888.

CHAPTER EIGHT

I looked like butchers, our coats and vests off, our shirt sleeves rolled up, and we were covered with blood. Oh it was an awful sight. . . . The shrieks and groans of the wounded were heart-rending. . . . The ram kept butting us and when Captain Flusser fell, the men seemed to lose heart, and we ran from the ram.

Having eliminated the threat of the Federal gunboats, Commander Cooke awaited Hoke's orders. The Confederate general sent word for the *Albemarle* to move close to shore and shell the Union fortifications. Under the combined army and naval assault, the Federal garrison managed to hold out only three days. On April 21, General Wessells surrendered his entire remaining force as well as 28 artillery pieces, 500 horses, 5,000 arms, and large quantities of supplies and ammunition.

The surrender struck a special fear into the Buffaloes of the Second Regiment North Carolina Union Volunteers. Many of them fled in terror by any means available once they learned that Wessells had surrendered. Those who took flight hid in the swamps and attempted to make their way to Washington or other Union lines. Others removed all evidence of their

During the Battle of Plymouth, the *Albemarle* (left front) rammed and sank the USS *Southfield* (right) and drove off the USS *Miami* (left rear). Engraving from R. U. Johnson and C. C. Buel, eds., *Battles and Leaders of the Civil War* (New York: Century Co., 1887-1888), 4: 628.

identity and assumed the names of killed soldiers in other Federal regiments. Those North Carolinians serving in Union ranks feared that if they were captured their Confederate captors would consider them traitors and execute them on the spot or perhaps hang them as had been done by Pickett's men at Kinston. Many of the Buffaloes who changed their names were sent to the dreaded prisoner-of-war camp at Andersonville and there carried their assumed names with them to the grave.

Like the Buffaloes, many African Americans trapped at the Battle of Plymouth were also the pathetic victims of Confederate atrocities. The Confederate soldiers refused to treat the black army recruits as prisoners of war and massacred many of them on sight. Numbers of those who fled into the swamps were hunted down and killed. A Confederate civilian in Plymouth recalled that "perhaps six hundred negroes and buffaloes . . . made for the nearest point of Peacock swamp. Three companies of cavalry and one of infantry were hunting them there all day, and nearly all were killed. I suppose no prisoners were taken." A Confederate officer observed that "several hundred negroes & negro officers attempted to escape when the town fell but were pursued & all most the last of them killed." A U.S. officer from Pennsylvania remembered after the war: "During the whole afternoon . . . we could hear the crack of rebel rifles along the swamps, where they were hunting down the colored troops and loyal North Carolinians. I heard a rebel Colonel say, with an oath, that they intended to shoot every Buffalo . . . and negro they found in our uniform." Black women and children also attempted to run away and were caught and remanded back into slavery.

The recapture of Plymouth made it possible for the town to serve as a port for the ironclad *Albemarle* to drive the U.S. gunboats from Albemarle and Pamlico Sounds. President Jefferson Davis was so pleased with Hoke's performance that he promoted him to the rank of major general. The seizure of Plymouth also enabled the Confederates to force the evacuation of the town of Washington. Before leaving that community, the U.S. troops plundered and burned many of its buildings. With the capture of Plymouth and Washington, Hoke turned his attention to New Bern. He called again for the *Albemarle*'s assistance, and Gen. P. G. T. Beauregard, who on April 23 had taken command of the Department of North Carolina and Southern Virginia, encouraged the use of the ironclad. In order to provide support at New Bern, the ram would have to cross Albemarle and Pamlico Sounds.

By May 4, 1864, Hoke had besieged New Bern and was confident that he would take the town even though the *Albemarle* had not yet arrived at the scene. At this time, Gen. Innis N. Palmer had replaced General Peck as the commander of the District of North Carolina and was in charge of the defense of New Bern. If Palmer would not surrender, vowed Hoke, he would launch a full assault on the town. But then Hoke received orders from Beauregard to report to Lee's Army of Northern Virginia then opposing the Federal assault being pressed forward by Gen. U. S. Grant toward Petersburg and Richmond. Hoke withdrew his troops northward into Virginia, and Confederate troops never again attacked New Bern in force.

In the meantime, the *Albemarle* had failed to reach New Bern. On May 5, the ironclad, along with the *Bombshell* and the *Cotton Plant*, started down the Roanoke River. But at the head of Albemarle Sound, they soon encountered a fleet of seven Union warships under the command of Capt. Melancton Smith. The U.S. vessels were the *Mattabesett*, *Sassacus*, *Wyalusing*, *Whitehead*, *Ceres*, *Commodore Hull*, and *Miami*. In the ensuing battle the *Sassacus* rammed the *Albemarle*, which heeled over and took on water. As the battle continued, the *Albemarle* sustained considerable damage. Fire from the Union vessels tore away her colors, damaged her steering mechanism, and so riddled her smokestack with holes that it was difficult to get up steam. Only when the crew threw butter, lard, and bacon into the boilers was the crippled ram able to manufacture enough steam to retreat back up the Roanoke to Plymouth.

Although damaged by the recent battle, the *Albemarle*, safely moored at Plymouth, still remained a threat to the Federals in the sound region. U.S. naval officers vowed that she had to be destroyed. For that task, they selected the daring Lt. William B. Cushing. A skeptical Assistant Secretary of the Navy Gustavus Fox authorized the young officer to proceed with a plan. Under the cover of darkness on October 27, Cushing with a party of men aboard a launch with a manned cutter in tow, steamed up the river to Plymouth, where the *Albemarle* lay at anchor, protected by a thirty-foot boom of logs. A fire on shore illuminated the ironclad. Upon approaching the light and being detected by a sentry on shore, Cushing ordered the cutter to cast off back downstream. On the launch, he called for full steam ahead, and, amid a hail of rifle fire from shore, his crew ran the launch onto the boom. Standing on the bow of the launch, his uniform riddled with bullet holes, Cushing calmly lowered a spar with a torpedo attached and exploded the device under the *Albemarle*. The ram immediately sank, with "a hole in her bottom big enough to drive a wagon." The Con-

With a daring nighttime raid in October 1864, Lt. William B. Cushing, USN, sank the *Albemarle*. Following the destruction of the ironclad, the Federals quickly recaptured Plymouth. Photograph from the State Archives.

federates captured the launch and most of the crew stranded on the boom. But the indomitable Cushing plunged into the water, swam to shore, and ultimately made his way to safety.

With the destruction of the *Albemarle*, the Federals quickly recaptured Plymouth on October 31 and soon reclaimed Washington as well. The destruction of the fearsome ironclad once again gave the United States dominance over the sound region.

Besides the *Albemarle*, the Confederacy had attempted to build other ironclads in North Carolina, but none ever achieved the success of that ram. At Kinston on the Neuse River, work had begun on the ironclad *Neuse*, and Hoke hoped that it would be ready in time to cooperate with the *Albemarle* in the attacks on Plymouth and New Bern. But delays in the construction prevented the vessel from participating in the Battle of Plymouth. The ram finally got under way to move down the Neuse River to aid in Hoke's assault on New Bern, but it grounded on a sandbar not far from Kinston and never saw action. The Confederates subsequently burned the *Neuse* to keep it from falling into Union hands.

To serve in conjunction with its other warships, the Confederate navy also built three ironclads for operations in the Wilmington area. In Wilmington shipyards in June 1862, construction began on the first two of these, the *Raleigh* and the *North Carolina* (originally the *Ladies Gunboat*). Those ironclads, similar in construction to the *Albemarle* and *Neuse*, were intended to serve as the nucleus of the Wilmington squadron. In May 1864 Secretary of the Navy Mallory also ordered the construction of a third ram, the *Wilmington*. In the previous month, the *Raleigh* had grounded on a sandbar and "broke its back" following an attack on the Federal blockading squadron at New Inlet. The *North Carolina* never became operational because of her faulty machinery. Infested with torpedo worms, she sprang a leak and sank at her moorings in September 1864. The *Wilmington* never reached completion, and the Confederates burned her when they evacuated Wilmington in February 1865.

For all practical purposes, Hoke's withdrawal to Virginia in May 1864 and the destruction of the *Albemarle* ended any further possibility for an effective Confederate counterattack in coastal North Carolina. Soon after those events, Federal raids resumed. One of the largest was an expedition near Kinston on December 10-15, 1864. By that time, the war had turned decisively against the Confederacy. All the Confederate army in coastal

North Carolina could do was remain on the defensive and hope either for a battlefield miracle elsewhere or for peace negotiations to end the conflict.

9 State Politics and the Home Front

As the Civil War raged and turned decidedly against the Confederacy, the pre-war reluctance to leave the Union felt in many areas of North Carolina, including the coastal counties, developed into a general dissatisfaction with the conflict and a desire for peace. That smoldering disgruntlement came to the forefront in the year 1863, when the resounding Confederate defeats at Vicksburg and Gettysburg proved the power and commitment of the Federal military. By that year, the Union army and navy had begun tightening their grip upon the Confederacy from the North and the West and along the Atlantic coast. The retreat of Lee's Army of Northern Virginia following the Battle of Antietam in Maryland in September 1862 and the subsequent issuance of the Emancipation Proclamation also ended any hope the South had of foreign intervention, especially from England, on behalf of the Confederate States of America.

Indications of North Carolinians' political moderation and reluctant attitude toward war appeared in the gubernatorial election of 1862. In that election, Zebulon B. Vance, the candidate of the Conservative Party who had originally opposed secession, defeated William Johnston, the candidate of the Confederate Party, which included many secessionists. Ultimately, it would be the fear of losing slavery and the social and economic revolution precipitated by that loss that would lead Vance and his like-minded fellow citizens to cling to the Confederacy long after they had become disenchanted with the war.

Much of that population's disenchantment was directed at the policies of the Confederate government. Conscription (drafting) of men into the Confederate army against their will excited much discontent among many North Carolinians. In fact, in coastal North Carolina some heads of households joined the ranks of the Buffaloes to remain near their families rather than be drafted into the Confederate army and sent away to fight. Other Confederate measures that angered Tar Heels were the tax-in-kind and impressment laws. The tax-in-kind law required a 10 percent tax on agricultural products. The impressment law allowed Confederate officers to impress food, forage, livestock, and other private property, as well as blacks (slave and free) for the war effort. Those policies, claimed North

Zebulon B. Vance became governor of North Carolina in September 1862 and served until the end of the war. Photograph from the State Archives.

Carolinians, were a violation of the doctrine of state rights. In the coastal counties, many inhabitants felt trapped in a no-man's-land where they suffered from having their crops, livestock, and slaves impressed by both Union and Confederate officers. In addition to impressment and tax-in-kind, shortages of essentials, speculation, inflation, and illegal distilling of corn and grain particularly rankled the poor. So too did the Twenty-Negro Act, which exempted from military service the owner or overseer of any plantation of twenty or more slaves. North Carolinians also resented Jefferson Davis's reluctance to appoint Confederate generals from North Carolina.

Davis had always been suspicious of the loyalty of North Carolina because of its slow response to calls for secession. Vance frequently quarreled with Davis over what the governor considered the president's discrimination against his state. Vance also protested the Confederate government's imposition of martial law, suspension of habeas corpus, and disregard of state laws.

As disillusionment with the war continued to grow, more North Carolinians began to favor peace negotiations with the U.S. government. Those persons found a spokesman in William W. Holden, editor of the *North Carolina Standard* in Raleigh. Holden organized peace meetings and called for peace negotiations with the Federals. Resolutions adopted at those meetings denounced Confederate despotism and advocated efforts to negotiate peace. North Carolinians loyal to the Confederate cause (members of the Confederate or Democratic Party) considered a peace movement as treason and an attempt to reconstruct the old Union. They demanded that Vance restrain Holden and his followers. President Davis also became concerned about Holden's activities. On July 24, he wrote Vance to ask if rumors were true that "Holden is engaged in the treasonable purpose of exciting the people of North Carolina to resistance against their government, and cooperation with the enemy."

Holden's activities also outraged some Confederate troops. In September

1863, Georgia troops traveling through Raleigh broke into the *Standard* office and scattered Holden's papers and the ink and type from his press. Holden's supporters in turn sacked the office of the *State Journal*, a Raleigh newspaper opposed to Holden. Alabama troops threatened to seize Holden, and the editor's friends declared they would protect him. Vance, with the cooperation of Davis and Confederate officers, managed to restore calm, and Holden abandoned for the time being his plans for peace overtures. But in November, the peace faction of the Conservative Party won six of the ten seats in the Confederate Congress, and Holden began calling for a state convention to initiate peace negotiations with the Union government. He promised to support Vance in the gubernatorial election of 1864 if Vance would endorse the convention. Vance, however, refused to support the convention, believing that despite its many disagreements with the Davis government, North Carolina should not seek a separate peace but remain in the Confederacy. To do otherwise, he felt, would pit North Carolina against the other states of the Confederacy and invite internal revolution, civil disorder, and bloodshed. He also was convinced that the survival of the Confederate States of America was the only way to ensure the survival of slavery. He would endorse only a peace that left slavery intact and acknowledged Confederate independence.

Because of Vance's position on peace, Holden decided to run against him in the 1864 election for governor. Vance won the election overwhelmingly, carrying all the North Carolina counties but three: Johnston, Randolph, and Wilkes. The last two were located in the so-called Quaker Belt, a Piedmont region of strong Unionism and peace sentiment. The total vote was 58,070 for Vance and 14,491 for Holden. In the coastal counties where Federal domination did not prevent the holding of state elections, the voters cast the majority of their votes for Vance.

With the reelection of Vance, North Carolinians found themselves facing eight more months of the hardships of war. No one was more aware of those hardships than the women of the Tar Heel State. Perhaps never before had there been a conflict in American history in which women played so substantive a role as they did in the Civil War. In the Confederacy, with its intrinsic shortage of white manpower, the role of women took on a particular significance. As early as 1862, the image of the noble and selfless Southern woman was already taking hold in the public imagination—an image of a woman who made willing sacrifices of husbands and sons for the good of the Southern cause, toiled long hours on the home front, taking care of children, the fields, the slaves, and wounded soldiers. The role of women in the Confederacy was much romanticized in the "Lost Cause" movement following the war. Still, it is nonetheless true that women in the Confederacy, including those in coastal North Carolina, played a significant wartime role.

Seventy-five percent of white men of military age across the South left home to go to war, leaving women with essential, and frequently unaccustomed, duties and responsibilities. With husbands and other male relatives away in the army, many female members of the planter aristocracy had to take charge of large plantations, including managing the production and sale of crops, supervising slaves and overseers, and other duties connected with maintaining a large agricultural enterprise. A larger class of women who lived on farms and small plantations (ten slaves or fewer) had to cope with even more strenuous duties than the planter's wives, for the physical demands of their labors were often greater than those of their wealthier sisters. At the bottom of the social scale were the women and their families who lived at a subsistence level and faced a real possibility of starvation when their men abandoned them for the army. Such families were known as "poor whites," or yeoman farmers. Poor land and health had always been their lot, and the war only worsened their marginal existence. In some urban areas—Salisbury and Raleigh, for example—poor women staged "bread riots," in an effort to secure food for their families and to protest the high prices of merchants, whom the women accused of speculation and extortion. County governments throughout the state established offices for providing relief to the destitute wives and children of soldiers. In coastal North Carolina, many of those women and their children flocked to Union lines seeking rations and other aid from the army and superintendent of the poor. At one point, Superintendent Vincent Colyer in New Bern reported that he was providing more relief to white refugees than to escaped slaves.

Despite the wartime strain and difficulties that at times seemed to overwhelm the women of coastal North Carolina, they persevered, fed and clothed their families, and in various capacities provided assistance to sick and wounded soldiers and the destitute. A number of women became nurses or aides in various hospitals. That represented a departure in social customs in many cases, for "up to that time," writes historian David A. Norris, "it had not been considered 'respectable' for women to make a profession of full-time hospital work." In October 1861, the state of North

Vincent Colyer, the Federal superintendent of the poor in New Bern, provided relief and medical care to black and white refugees. Engraving from *The National Cyclopedia of American Biography* (New York: James T. White and Co., 1898–), 7:541.

Carolina opened the First North Carolina Hospital in Petersburg, Virginia, on Perry Street, near the Wilmington and Weldon Railroad. Several coastal North Carolina women held important jobs at that facility. Among them were Catherine Kennedy of Wilmington, head matron, and Mary Pettigrew, Nannie Beckwith, and "Mrs. Beasley of Plymouth," assistant matrons.

At the First North Carolina Hospital and field hospitals throughout the Confederacy, the bulk of the patient care was the responsibility of a male steward. Stewards usually were proficient in pharmacy and oversaw the cleanliness of the ward and inventoried medical supplies in addition to their direct patient care duties. At first, hospitals in the Tar Heel State were under the supervision of the North Carolina Medical Department with its own surgeon general. But eventually the Confederate government was operating most of the hospitals in the state. In the fall of 1862, the Confederate Congress authorized that two matrons were to be assigned to each field hospital to oversee the "domestic economy" of the facility. The Confederate government soon observed that hospitals employing female matrons had a significantly lower mortality rate than those without female staff. Throughout the war, however, few upper- and middle-class women worked in the hospitals. The task of taking care of men's bodies was left primarily to men, slaves, and poor white women. In coastal North Carolina, the Federals operated a general hospital at New Bern, and the Confederates had one there prior to Burnside's capture of the town. At Wilmington, the Confederates had a general hospital opened by April 1862. Also accessible to the coastal area were two Confederate general hospitals at Goldsboro. A temporary hospital at Elizabeth City had cared for the Confederate wounded from the Battle of Roanoke Island in February 1862.

During the war the so-called wayside hospitals appeared in coastal North Carolina. Those small hospitals were located mostly along the Wilmington and Weldon Railroad. Originally operated by volunteers, many of whom were women, the wayside hospitals provided medical assistance to wounded and other convalescent soldiers traveling to and from the Virginia battlefields on the train. By August 1862 Wilmington had a wayside hospital with the local women volunteering their services and the town's civilian physicians tending the sick and wounded. Weldon and Goldsboro, too, had busy wayside hospitals.

Women also formed soldiers' aid societies. A rare handwritten ledger for a New Bern society resides at the Museum of the Confederacy in Richmond. The following excerpt describes the society's establishment and mission:

> Soldiers' relief society: at a meeting of the ladies of New Bern held at Lowthrop Hall on Tuesday the 3rd of September [1861], for the purpose of providing suitable food and nourishment for the sick soldiers now encamped in about this town, Mrs. Richard N. Taylor having been chosen president, Miss Nannie Davis secretary, and Mrs. J. M. F. Harrison treasurer, the following preamble

and resolutions were adopted:

Whereas it has been represented to us that several soldiers in the camps in and around New Bern are sick, and that they require attention and nourishing food in order to facilitate their recovery, therefore,

Resolved, that this association which shall be called the Soldiers' Relief Society deems it due to the gallant defenders of our southern homes that they should receive proper care and attention during sickness, and that the ladies of New Bern do hereby cheerfully assume that duty.

The resolution went on to state that New Bern would be divided into districts, with a certain number of ladies assigned to each to see to needs of soldiers within that district. Managers for each area would be appointed and contributions solicited for money and such provisions as butter, poultry, eggs, and milk. The society resolved to send copies of its regular proceedings to the New Bern *Daily Progress* for publication.

An entry in the society's ledger on September 14 proudly noted the donation of fifty chickens, as well as the good news that ninety patients at the hospital at the fairgrounds had recovered sufficiently to be discharged. But an entry on October 3 indicated that the demands from the hospital were becoming too large a burden on the society. Consequently, "the society passed a resolution that their purpose was to care for the sick *and not to feed the army as a whole*, and would have to limit their efforts strictly to the very sick in the future, and not to everyone in the hospital in general." The New Bern ladies' ledger ended with its entry of February 20, 1862, in which it recorded that a group called the Confederate Minstrels gave a concert to benefit sick soldiers and donated their proceeds, $59.50, to the society. Public relief efforts for Confederate soldiers soon ended in New Bern when Burnside's troops captured and occupied the town.

Black women also formed their own clubs or societies to support their men serving in the Federal ranks. As noted earlier, when troops of the African Brigade left New Bern in July 1863 for duty in South Carolina, they proudly carried a beautiful banner that they had been presented by the Colored Ladies Union Relief Association, which had collected funds for the banner "from their own people" in New Bern. African American women in the Federally occupied towns or freedmen settlements of coastal North Carolina struggled in the same way as their white counterparts to support their families on their own while their husbands, sons, and other male relatives served in the Union army. In addition to receiving any rations or other aid provided by the Federals, black women earned extra income by working for the U.S. Army as servants, hospital aides, cooks, laundresses, and seamstresses. One African American woman, Rachel Thomas, who resided in the Trent River Settlement at New Bern, became a schoolteacher at the settlement after being educated by white New England female teachers who operated a school in the camp. During Reconstruction, Thomas established her own school at the settlement and was hired by the American Freedmen's Union Commission of New York to teach there. Many of the idealistic New England women who came to coastal North Carolina to teach the newly liberated African Americans were members of the American Missionary Association or other Northern philanthropic organizations. The Civil War made it possible for a large number of women to enter the profession of teaching, which before the conflict had been primarily the province of men.

Part of the popular lore about the Civil War are the tales of Southern women who served as spies or smuggled important messages and mail behind Union lines. One such daring female was Miss Emmeline Pigott of Beaufort, "who barely escaped being shot as a spy." Mrs. Alexander Taylor of New Bern is said to have bewildered slow-witted Union officers as she smuggled mail to Confederate prisoners of war in New Bern. Mrs. Taylor, nicknamed "The Prison Mother," reportedly also brought food and comfort to the prisoners. According to legend, Mrs. Elizabeth Carraway Howland provided Confederates with plans of Union fortifications as they were being built at New Bern. "She would," as the story goes, "secret the paper in a small roll inside the bone of the ham which her daughter and son carried down the river to the Confederates." Mrs. Julius Lewis kept Federal officers billeted in her house in New Bern, but local tradition has it that her hospitality hid the fact that she relayed the conversations she overheard in her home to Confederate troops outside the town. To obtain information on Union strength at New Bern for General Lee, Mrs. A. M. Meekins, "disguised as a country woman with a bale of cotton to sell," is said to have walked past U.S. sentries, "secured the desired information and past [sic] safely back through Union lines." One unfortunate New Bern belle allegedly was held hostage by the Federals and "almost choked to death by 'bummers'" but managed to frighten away Union soldiers who were trying to dig up the graves of her ancestors.

Foster General Hospital complex, where the majority of the Union army's yellow fever cases were treated during the New Bern epidemic of 1864. Photograph from the U.S. Army Military History Institute.

Although some of the tales about women in coastal North Carolina during the war might be open to skepticism, the hardships faced by women and their families were only too real. Shortages of food, salt, sugar, clothing, shoes, leather, and cotton and wool and the cards to make those fabrics plagued the home-front populace throughout the war. Sickness and disease also posed a serious threat to the population. The crowding of refugees and escaped slaves into coastal towns and freedmen's camps resulted in poor sanitation and stimulated the spread of communicable diseases such as measles, smallpox, typhoid, and other maladies. Mortality rates were generally high in the crowded towns and camps. As already noted, Vincent Colyer had fugitive slaves vaccinated for smallpox and created a hospital for them in New Bern.

Late in the summer of 1862, a yellow fever epidemic occurred in Wilmington. The disease presumably was brought to the port city from the Bahamas aboard the blockade-runner *Kate*. The first recorded death was that of German immigrant Lewis Swarzman on September 9. Eventually the city began to burn tar or rosin on its streets to prevent the spread of the disease, for at the time authorities believed that yellow fever was an airborne disease. (Only later would medical science determine that yellow fever was actually transmitted by the female *Aedes aegypti* mosquito.) By the third week in September, the epidemic raged in Wilmington. Nearby communities refused to harbor refugees from Wilmington out of fear for their own health. By early October, there had been almost four hundred cases of yellow fever in town and forty confirmed deaths. The unseasonably warm eighty-degree days in October allowed the vector mosquitoes to continue their work unabated. A sudden shift toward cold temperatures then produced a plethora of pneumonia cases in those debilitated by yellow fever. The drop in temperature did, however, stop the spread of the disease. By early November, the epidemic was over, with 1,500 persons having fallen ill and almost 700 having died, fatalities that accounted for almost 15 percent of the total population of Wilmington. As a result of the outbreak of yellow fever, all blockade-runners coming into the port were required to be quarantined for weeks before their crews could come ashore. In August 1864, yellow fever broke out in New Bern and raged until November, claiming several hundred soldiers and civilians.

As the war continued into the fall of 1864 and home-front conditions worsened throughout much of the Tar Heel State, many coastal North Carolinians longed for an end to the conflict. But those inhabitants still loyal to the Confederacy held on in the hope of a favorable peace settlement if Lincoln failed to be reelected in the presidential election in November. Lincoln, however, was reelected, which ensured that the Federal government would continue its relentless assault into the heartland of the Confederacy. When news of Lincoln's reelection reached the coastal counties, many residents realized that a Federal victory and an end to the war were not too far in the future.

10 The Fall of Fort Fisher and Wilmington

Of the many steam blockade-runners that entered North Carolina waters from December 1861 to December 1864, a number of them were vessels that made the trip several times. The *Banshee*, for example, made seven voyages into Wilmington from Nassau before being captured while attempting to enter the North Carolina port on November 21, 1863. In fact, as the number of trips made by blockade-runners increased, so did the chances of being caught by Federal blockaders. All the steam blockade-runners that came to North Carolina during the period December 1861-December 1864 departed from either Nassau or Bermuda, and all entered the port of Wilmington except for the *Nashville*, which entered Beaufort from Bermuda on February 28, 1862.

By the fall of 1864, Wilmington had become the most important seaport in the Confederacy. Trapped in the trenches at Petersburg, Gen. Robert E. Lee relied almost exclusively on the supplies from the North Carolina port, via the Wilmington and Weldon Railroad, to sustain his army. The Federal

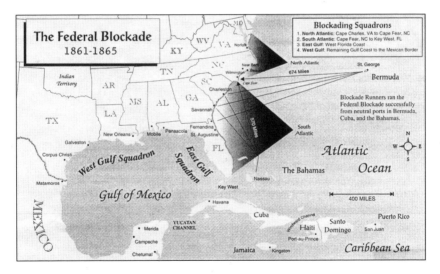

Map from Mark A. Moore, *Moore's Historical Guide to the Wilmington Campaign and the Battles for Fort Fisher* (Mason City, Iowa: Savas Publishing Co., 1999), 4. Reproduced by permission of the author.

occupation of coastal North Carolina had denied Lee the rich agricultural produce of much of the region, and he needed the supplies that came through the blockade at Wilmington. Furthermore, blockade-running activity had been seriously curtailed at the port of Charleston, South Carolina, since July 1863, when a Union attack secured islands near the harbor and managed to establish artillery positions that controlled much of the harbor channel. That control plus increased Federal naval surveillance virtually closed the port of Charleston to blockade-runners. As a result, most of the Charleston blockade-running companies moved their operations to Wilmington, which "inherited the entire East Coast trade." Even the Confederacy's secret agents operated out of Wilmington. The famous female agent Rose O'Neal Greenhow drowned when her blockade-runner, *Condor*, ran aground near New Inlet in September 1864. Subsequently she was buried with military honors in a Wilmington cemetery.

Located twenty-eight miles up the Cape Fear River, Wilmington was ideal for blockade-running. Protected from enemy bombardment by Confederate forts at the mouth of the river, the port could be accessed by two entrances to the Cape Fear River. Those inlets were separated by Smith's Island, which was located directly in the mouth of the river. North of the island was New Inlet and south was Old Inlet, and the distance separating them was only six miles. Between the inlets, Frying Pan Shoals jutted out into the

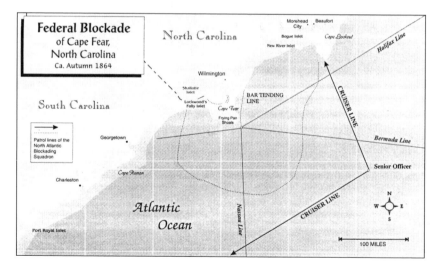

Map from Moore's *Historical Guide to the Wilmington Campaign and the Battles for Fort Fisher*, 4. Reproduced by permission of the author.

CHAPTER TEN

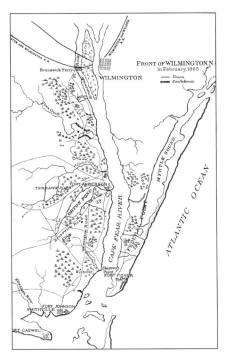

This map shows Wilmington and the defenses of Cape Fear, including the formidable Fort Fisher. From Walter Clark, ed., *The Histories of the Several Regiments and Battalions from North Carolina in the Great War, 1861-'65* (Raleigh: State of N.C., 1901), 5: following 226.

Atlantic for about twenty-five miles. Consequently, ships attempting to blockade the two channels had to cover a fifty-mile arc and simultaneously stay out of range of Confederate shore batteries. The formidable Confederate Goliath of Fort Fisher protected New Inlet, which was the preferred entrance for most blockade-runners. Forts Caswell and Campbell guarded Old Inlet. Fort Holmes stood on Smith's Island, and up the river on the west bank at Smithville and Old Brunswick Town were Forts Johnston and Anderson respectively.

When the war began, blockading any Southern port was a difficult task, and blockading one such as Wilmington was virtually impossible. The U.S. Department of the Navy had only forty-two ships when the conflict began, and in May 1861 only two ships guarded the entire North Carolina coast. It was July before the first blockader, the *Daylight*, arrived off the mouth of the Cape Fear River. Even after the Federal navy had a sizable cordon of ships guarding against clandestine vessels attempting to enter the port of Wilmington, many blockade-runners continued to slip past the blockade.

Perhaps the best known of the blockade-runners operating out of Wilmington was the steamer *Advance*, which was owned by the state of North Carolina. Shortly after he took office in 1862, Governor Vance authorized the purchase of a vessel and supplies. Vance selected John White as the state's purchasing agent in England and appointed Capt. Thomas M. Crossan to locate and purchase a suitable ship for blockade-running. Crossan decided on an English vessel named the *Lord Clyde*, which he

On board the blockade-runner *Lillian* as she runs into the port of Wilmington. Photograph of engraving from the State Archives.

bought and renamed the *Advance*. At around the same time, White employed the English company Alexander Collie and Company to operate as agents for North Carolina to secure supplies for shipment through the blockade. The *Advance* made her first successful run into Wilmington in June 1863 and completed a number of trips before being captured in the summer of 1864.

In addition to the blockade-runners, two Confederate commerce raiders operated out of the port of Wilmington near the end of the war. On August 6, 1864, the *Tallahassee* (formerly the blockade-runner *Atalanta*), under the command of Lt. John Taylor Wood, ran the blockade and steamed as far north as Nova Scotia. She destroyed twenty-six Federal ships, boarded five others, and released two before slipping back through the blockade into Wilmington on August 26. At the end of October, the *Tallahassee*, renamed the *Olustee*, and another raider, the *Chickamauga* (formerly the blockade-runner *Edith*), passed through heavy gunfire from the Federal blockading fleet and began preying upon U.S. ships along the East Coast from Wilmington to Halifax as a number of Union ships pursued them. The

CHAPTER TEN

The Confederate spy Rose O'Neal Greenhow drowned in September 1864
when the blockade-runner *Condor* ran aground at Cape Fear. Greenhow
was returning from Europe, where she had placed her daughter (left)
in a convent. The female spy is buried in Wilmington. Photograph
from the State Archives.

Chickamauga destroyed six Union ships and returned to Wilmington on
November 19. The *Olustee* sank seven vessels off the coast of Delaware
before running back into the Cape Fear River ahead of the pursuit and
heavy fire by several Union warships on November 6.

On September 2, 1864, the U.S. War Department agreed to a joint operation with the navy to close the port of Wilmington. Secretary of the Navy

Gideon Welles had been urging a "cojoint attack upon Wilmington for months" and was convinced that if the port could be captured "it would be almost as important as the capture of Richmond on the fate of the Rebels." But achieving such an objective would not be easy, for the key to capturing Wilmington was to take the formidable Fort Fisher, an extremely well fortified and armed position.

Work had begun on Fort Fisher in April 1861. In July 1862 the Confederate engineering officer Col. William Lamb had taken command of constructing the fortifications. With construction under his direction, Fort Fisher eventually could claim the largest earthworks in the Confederacy and one of the largest in the world. The labor of many slaves and conscripts helped make the site almost impregnable. The fort was shaped like an L, with its long side toward the ocean and its short side facing north across a narrow peninsula. Sandbagged and revetted walls were twenty feet high and twenty-five feet thick. Forty-eight guns armed the fortifications, and heavy traverses between the gun chambers provided protection for gunners from enemy bombardment. Soldiers could take refuge in bombproof shelters within the fort. A ditch, palisades, and a mine field also guarded the fort from land attack from the north.

In late December 1864, a combined U.S. Army and Navy expedition appeared off Cape Fear. In command of the navy was Rear Adm. David D. Porter, and Gen. Benjamin F. Butler commanded the army contingent, a detachment from his Army of the James. For the Confederates, Gen. Braxton Bragg had taken over the district command from Gen. William H. C. Whiting, who then took direct charge of Wilmington's defenses. Colonel Lamb commanded at Fort Fisher. The Federals began their attack on the night of the twenty-third, when sailors, following a bizarre plan conceived by General Butler, towed an old ship filled with gunpowder and other explosives within several hundred yards of the fort. The vessel exploded on the twenty-fourth after drifting back toward the Union fleet. Apparently Butler believed that such a blast would do great damage to the fort, but the explosion had no effect. On Christmas Day, Federal sailors leveled a tremendous naval bombardment at the fort in preparation for an attack by Butler's troops who had landed north of the fort. But Fort Fisher suffered very little damage as the defenders crouched in their bombproof shelters. In the meantime, three thousand army troops under the command of Butler's chief lieutenant, Maj. Gen. Godfrey Weitzel, had landed on the beach north of the fort and began moving south for a land assault

Admiral David D. Porter, officer in charge of the North Atlantic Blockading Squadron, commanded the naval attacks on Fort Fisher. Photograph from the State Archives.

on the fort. Weitzel advanced his skirmish line within fifty yards of the Confederate fortifications, but General Butler suddenly lost his nerve, ordered a retreat, and called for the troops to re-embark on the transports. He acted in such haste that he left a detachment of men still on the beach,

Armstrong Rifle at Fort Fisher. Photograph from the State Archives.

and on the following day, Admiral Porter ordered a vessel to evacuate the stranded men. Thus ended the first Union attempt to capture Fort Fisher.

Despite the failure of the first attempt, Admiral Porter remained sure that the "Gibraltar of the Confederacy" could be taken, and he requested the return of the army assault force but with a new general to replace Butler. Gen. U. S. Grant assigned Brig. Gen. Alfred H. Terry to lead the Federal troops in a new attack. On January 12, 1865, the U.S. armada was once again visible off Fort Fisher. On the following day the naval guns initiated a tremendous bombardment, this time concentrating on the land face of the fort. General Terry also began landing his troops totaling ninety-six hundred men, including a contingent of sailors and marines and two brigades of black soldiers. The troops entrenched themselves behind a breastwork and on the fourteenth pushed forward to investigate the land front a few hundred yards from the fort's parapet. General Terry decided to launch his attack on the fifteenth.

Unfortunately for Colonel Lamb and his men in the fort, who had been joined by General Whiting, General Bragg would not commit to the defense of Fort Fisher the thousands of troops—commanded by Gen. Robert F. Hoke—bivouacked at Sugar Loaf, a defensive position between

CHAPTER TEN

Gun traverse at Fort Fisher. Photograph from the State Archives.

the fort and Wilmington. Lamb received only a few reinforcements, and he had only about twelve hundred men to defend his works. On the morning of the fifteenth, the Union ships offshore began raining down a tremendous fire of an estimated one hundred shells a minute on the fort. On the beach, the detachment of about two thousand sailors and marines prepared to assault the northeast salient of the Confederate bastion. The sailors were armed with cutlasses and pistols, and the marines were to support them with musket fire. On the west side of the peninsula, an army division led by Maj. Gen. Adelbert Ames formed to attack the fort at its western end. Terry's remaining troops, mostly the African American regiments, guarded the Federals' rear defensive line, which ran across the peninsula from the ocean to the Cape Fear River.

In mid-afternoon, the navy ceased its bombardment of the fort, and the Confederate defenders braced themselves for the land attack. As the sailors and marines charged the northeast corner of the fort, Lamb's grapeshot and canister tore into their ranks and forced them to retreat in panic. But on the west side of the fort, Ames's men gained the parapet. The Confederates counterattacked in savage hand-to-hand fighting, and Colonel Lamb ordered his guns to swivel and fire into the blue ranks. General Whiting was wounded during the fierce fighting. For a time it appeared that the Confederates would drive the Union troops from their

Union troops assault Fort Fisher. Engraving from *Harper's Weekly*, 1865.

works. But then the U.S. naval guns, which had already resumed firing upon the ocean-front fortifications, began leveling a precise and devastating fire on the land-front works. Although risky because it might also hit Union troops, this bombardment turned the tide of the battle.

CHAPTER TEN

Following the fall of Fort Fisher on January 15, 1865, the USS *Lenapee* supported the advance of Federal land troops upon the town of Wilmington. Photograph from the State Archives.

The U.S. naval guns continued to pound the fort with accuracy and effect. The Confederates retreated back through their fortifications as the Union soldiers pressed them. While trying to lead a desperate counter-charge, Colonel Lamb was wounded by a bullet to his hip. Confederate command then passed to Maj. James Reilly, who led the retreat from the fort toward Battery Buchanan, located south of the fort near the tip of the peninsula. There Reilly hoped to re-form his troops and re-engage the enemy. He soon learned that the men in Battery Buchanan had already abandoned their post after they spiked their guns. At the same time, the Federal brigade of Brig. Gen. Joseph C. Abbott and the Twenty-seventh Regiment United States Colored Troops were bearing down from the north. Seeing the hopelessness of his situation, Reilly surrendered to the first company of the Federal advance. The major had transported Colonel Lamb and General Whiting to Fort Buchanan on stretchers, and in the late evening of January 15, 1865, General Whiting formally surrendered Fort Fisher to General Terry. Whiting later died of dysentery in a Federal prison. Lamb was sent to the Federal prison at Fort Monroe and after a number of years fully recovered from his wound. He died in 1900.

The total number of casualties for the battles of Fort Fisher is difficult to determine. But the Federal casualties for both engagements probably totaled about 1,548 and those of the Confederates about 2,289. According to one authority on the battles of Fort Fisher, Mark A. Moore, "The Federal infantry attack on January 15, 1865, initiated perhaps the most prolonged hand-to-hand engagement of the Civil War. The close-quarters nature of the fight, together with the unprecedented bombardment from the Federal fleet, produced casualties of an unusually grave character. Considering the amount of ordnance expended upon the fort, it is a wonder that the number of killed and wounded . . . was not much greater." The collapse of Fort Fisher, of course, ended Wilmington's role as a blockade-running port and cut the final lifeline of the Confederacy.

With the loss of Fort Fisher, the Confederates had to abandon the other defenses near the mouth of the Cape Fear River. They demolished Forts Caswell, Campbell, Holmes, and Johnston and then marched up the west bank of the Cape Fear to Fort Anderson. Directly across the river, General Hoke's troops remained entrenched at Sugar Loaf. From these positions, General Bragg attempted to hold the city of Wilmington. His superiors in Richmond wanted to prevent the Federals from capturing the port and using it to supply the army of General Sherman entering the Carolinas from the south. Within about a month, however, a joint Union operation would be under way to take Wilmington.

With U.S. soldiers occupying the abandoned Confederate defensive works on the Cape Fear peninsula, General Terry and Admiral Porter awaited the reinforcements they felt they needed to take Wilmington. Late in January, General Grant arrived from Virginia to discuss future operations around Wilmington with Terry and Porter. Grant supported Sherman's plan to march northward into the Carolinas, and he wanted to ensure that Sherman had a base of supply at Goldsboro as he struck into the heart of the Tar Heel State. Wilmington, Grant reasoned, could be the port for supplying Goldsboro. The railroad from Wilmington was still operational, and a capture of Wilmington would gain control of the railroad, which could serve as a supply line for Sherman. Terry and Porter recommended to Grant that Federal land forces attack Wilmington from west of the Cape Fear River, where they would have plenty of room to maneuver as they advanced on the city from Smithville via Fort Anderson. Other troops could move on the Confederate defenses on the peninsula east of the Cape Fear River, and Porter's gunboats could provide support from the river. Grant agreed to the plan before returning to Virginia, and he ordered to the Cape Fear area Gen. John M. Schofield and his Twenty-third Corps, Army of the Ohio, which had been with the Union army in Tennessee. The War Depart-

Wilmington surrendered on February 22, 1865. Photograph of engraving of the town from the State Archives.

ment re-established the Department of North Carolina with Schofield as its commander. His mission was to take command of the Wilmington campaign and then drive toward Goldsboro to join and resupply Sherman. A unit commanded by Brig. Gen. Thomas F. Meagher had been detached from Sherman's army and sent to New Bern. That force had orders to advance to Goldsboro simultaneously with Schofield's troops after Wilmington had been captured.

On February 11, 1865, General Schofield tested the Confederate line at Sugar Loaf by advancing Terry's men. Hoke's defenses, however, held, and Schofield then launched a drive up the west side of the Cape Fear River toward Wilmington. A division under the command of Gen. Jacob D. Cox led the advance, which was supported by Porter's gunboats on the river. The Federals' first objective was Fort Anderson under the command of Gen. Johnson C. Hagood. As the Union troops surrounded the fort on the morning of February 19, Hagood and his men abandoned their works and retreated to Wilmington. Hoke's troops also abandoned Sugar Loaf and withdrew up the peninsula. The Confederates fought delaying actions, but by the evening of February 21, the Federals were at the outskirts of Wilmington. General Bragg gave orders to abandon the city and for Hoke and Hagood to leave their defensive line and withdraw to the north. Before fleeing, the Confederates set afire many supplies and several ships at dock to prevent their falling into the hands of the enemy. A crew took the *Chickamauga* upriver and scuttled her, and a detail destroyed a railroad bridge across the Cape Fear River.

At around midmorning on February 22, 1865, Mayor John Dawson stood in front of the Wilmington city hall awaiting the arrival of General Terry, who would accept the city's surrender. Soon the mayor heard a military band in the distance, then saw blue columns approaching. General Terry and his staff rode up on horseback and dismounted. The general and the mayor entered city hall to prepare the formal surrender of the last coastal bastion of the Confederacy.

EPILOGUE: *The War Ends*

After he captured Wilmington, General Schofield discovered that he had at that port few railroad cars or wagons with which to transport supplies to Goldsboro for his rendezvous with Sherman. He therefore sent reinforcements to New Bern and planned to begin his trek inland from that point. He ordered General Cox to take command at New Bern and "push forward at once" toward Goldsboro.

Cox began moving two divisions, with one division to follow, on March 6. On the following day his vanguard clashed with Bragg's retreating Confederates who had made a stand at Southwest Creek, east of Kinston. Here Bragg, whose army included the commands of Generals Hoke and D. H. Hill, hoped to halt or at least delay the Union advance to Goldsboro. The wagon roads from New Bern, the road from Wilmington, and the Atlantic and North Carolina Railroad all crossed Southwest Creek. In the ensuing battle, known as the Battle of Wise's Forks, Bragg's men managed to drive back the Federals but failed to turn the enemy flanks.

Reinforced from New Bern and Wilmington, Schofield's divisions carried the field on March 10, and Bragg withdrew his troops to Kinston and then Goldsboro, where he awaited orders from Gen. Joseph E. Johnston. Johnston at that point was in command of the Confederate forces in the North Carolina district, which included remnants of the Army of Tennessee. On March 8, 1865, Sherman crossed the line into North Carolina and began moving toward Fayetteville, which he reached on March 11. Four days later, his troops crossed the Cape Fear River en route to Goldsboro. As he waited to see in which direction Sherman might march, General Johnston concentrated his forces at Smithfield. On March 16, a part of Johnston's army commanded by Lt. Gen. William J. Hardee fought with a wing of Sherman's expedition at Averasboro. Although the battle was small and indecisive, it nevertheless had the effect of dividing or spreading out Sherman's army. That outcome gave Johnston an open opportunity on March 19 to strike Sherman while he was vulnerable near Bentonville, a small town west of Goldsboro. For a while the Confederates seemed to be winning the Battle of Bentonville, the largest battle of the war fought in North Carolina, but Union reinforcements began arriving on the

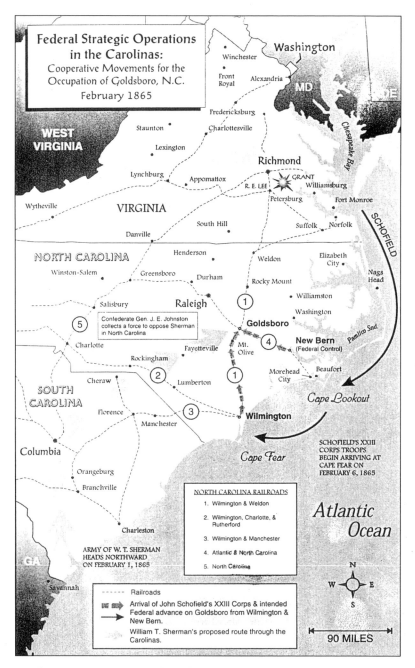

Map from *Moore's Historic Guide to the Wilmington Campaign and the Battles for Fort Fisher*, 94. Reproduced by permission of the author.

twentieth. By March 21, Sherman had his entire army at Bentonville, and that night Johnston withdrew to Smithfield. Sherman continued on to Goldsboro, where he found awaiting him the Union troops from Wilmington and New Bern along with General Schofield.

At Goldsboro, Sherman discovered that the railroad from the coast had not been repaired and needed supplies had not yet arrived. By March 24, however, the Federals had repaired the track from New Bern, and the first train had arrived in Goldsboro from that coastal town. On the twenty-fifth, Sherman left North Carolina for City Point, Virginia, to confer with General Grant about further operations. In the meantime, another Union general, George Stoneman, and six thousand cavalrymen had invaded the state from east Tennessee and begun raiding western North Carolina, wreaking havoc as they moved.

Sherman returned to Goldsboro on March 30, and on April 6 he learned that Richmond had fallen. Grant telegraphed him that "the rebel armies are now the only strategic points." Sherman then issued orders making the capture of Raleigh and the capitulation of Johnston's army the remaining objectives of his expedition. On April 11, Johnston, who was in Raleigh, received a telegram from President Davis ordering Johnston to meet the president and his cabinet at Greensboro. Johnston boarded a train for Greensboro around midnight and on the morning of the twelfth met with Davis and his cabinet and confirmed the surrender of Lee's army at Appomattox on April 9. In the meantime, Johnston's troops, whom he had left in the command of General Hardee, evacuated Raleigh. On April 13, Sherman's troops occupied the capital city. Governor Vance had already departed to meet with President Davis, with whom he eventually managed to connect in Charlotte. Vance's representatives, William A. Graham and David L. Swain, both influential political leaders and former governors, had negotiated with Sherman the terms of Raleigh's surrender.

In the meantime, President Davis had authorized Johnston to discuss with Sherman the suspension of hostilities. Johnston returned to his army, which was then moving toward Greensboro. On April 14, he sent a message to Sherman asking for a cessation of hostilities. That communication led to a meeting between Sherman and Johnston at the James Bennett farmhouse near Durham. There surrender negotiations took place on April 17-18. Sherman initially granted generous terms to Johnston, but they were rejected by the War Department in Washington. The two generals then met again at the Bennett house on April 26, and Johnston agreed to terms similar to those granted to Lee at Appomattox. That agreement effectively ended the Civil War, although some skirmishing in areas of the Confederacy would continue for a few weeks until news of surrender was received.

The last shots fired in North Carolina occurred near the western town of Waynesville in early May 1865. With that volley, the long four years of combat that had begun with the coastal battle of Hatteras in 1861 came to a conclusion in the Tar Heel State.

Bibliography

Alexander, John, and James Lazell. *Ribbon of Sand: The Amazing Convergence of the Ocean and the Outer Banks.* Chapel Hill: Algonquin Books, 1992.

Anderson, Bern. *By Sea and by River: The Naval History of the Civil War.* New York: Knopf, 1962.

Anderson, Lucy L. *North Carolina Women of the Confederacy.* Fayetteville, N.C.: United Daughters of the Confederacy, 1926.

Barrett, John G. *The Civil War in North Carolina.* Chapel Hill: University of North Carolina Press, 1963.

————. *Sherman's March through the Carolinas.* Chapel Hill: University of North Carolina Press, 1956.

Barry, Richard S. "Fort Macon: Its History." *North Carolina Historical Review* 27 (April 1950): 163-170.

Beale, C. H. "The First Confederate Flag on the Atlantic." *Confederate Veteran* 15 (May 1907): 227-228.

Black, Robert C. *The Railroads of the Confederacy.* Chapel Hill: University of North Carolina Press, 1952.Black, Wilfred W. "Civil War Letters of E. N. Boots from New Bern and Plymouth." *North Carolina Historical Review* 36 (April 1959): 205-223.

Browning, Judkin J. "'Little Souled Mercenaries'? The Buffaloes of Eastern North Carolina during the Civil War." *North Carolina Historical Review* 77 (July 2000): 337-363.

Browning, Robert M., Jr. *From Cape Charles to Cape Fear: The North Atlantic Blockading Squadron during the Civil War.* Tuscaloosa: University of Alabama Press, 1993.

Butler, Lindley S. and Alan D. Watson, eds. *The North Carolina Experience: An Interpretive and Documentary History.* Chapel Hill: University of North Carolina Press, 1984.

Butler, Lindley S. *Pirates, Privateers, and Rebel Raiders of the Carolina Coast.* Chapel Hill: University of North Carolina Press, 2000.

Carse, Robert. *Blockade: The Civil War at Sea.* New York: Rinehart, 1958.

Cheney, John L., Jr., ed. *North Carolina Government, 1585-1979: A Narrative and Statistical History.* Raleigh: Department of the Secretary of State, 1981.

Civil War Naval Chronology, 1861-1865. Washington, D.C.: Naval History Division, Navy Department, 1971.

Clark, Walter, ed. *The Histories of the Several Regiments and Battalions from North Carolina in the Great War, 1861-'65.* 5 vols. Raleigh: State of North Carolina, 1901.

Cochran, Hamilton. *Blockade Runners of the Confederacy.* Indianapolis: Bobbs-Merrill Co., 1958.

Crofts, Daniel. *Reluctant Confederates: Upper South Unionists in the Secession Crisis.* Chapel Hill: University of North Carolina Press, 1989.

Current, Richard M., et al., eds. *Encyclopedia of the Confederacy.* 5 vols. New York: Simon and Schuster, 1993.

Degler, Carl N. *The Other South: Southern Dissenters in the Nineteenth Century.* New York: Harper and Row, 1974.

Delany, Norman C. "Charles Henry Foster and the Unionists of Eastern North Carolina." *North Carolina Historical Review* 37 (July 1960): 348-366.

Derby, William P. *Bearing Arms in the Twenty-seventh Massachusetts Regiment of Volunteer Infantry during the Civil War, 1861-1865.* Boston: Wright and Potter Co., 1883.

Dix, Mary S. "'And Three Rousing Cheers for the Privates': A Diary of the 1862 Roanoke Island Expedition." *North Carolina Historical Review* 71 (January 1994): 62-84.

Dowdey, Clifford, and Louis H. Manarin, eds. *The Wartime Papers of R. E. Lee.* Boston: Little, Brown, 1961.

Dunbar, Gary. *The Historical Geography of the North Carolina Outer Banks.* Baton Rouge: Louisiana State University Press, 1958.

Elliott, Robert G. *Ironclad of the Roanoke: Gilbert Elliott's Albemarle.* Shippensburg, Pa.: White Mane Publishing Co., 1994.

Escott, Paul D. *After Secession: Jefferson Davis and the Failure of Confederate Nationalism.* Baton Rouge: Louisiana State University Press, 1978.

Evans, Clement, A., ed. *Confederate Military History: A Library of Confederate States History . . . Written by Distinguished Men of the South.* 12 vols. Atlanta: Confederate Publishing Co., 1899.

Farnham, Thomas J., and Francis P. King. "'The March of the Destroyer': The New Bern Yellow Fever Epidemic of 1864." *North Carolina Historical Review* 73 (October 1996): 435-483.

Faust, Patricia L., et al., eds. *Historical Times Illustrated Encyclopedia of the Civil War.* New York: HarperCollins, 1991.

Goff, Richard D. *Confederate Supply.* Durham: Duke University Press, 1969.

Gragg, Rod. *Confederate Goliath: The Battle of Fort Fisher.* New York: HarperCollins, 1991.

Halleck, Henry W. *Elements of Military Art and Science.* New York: Appleton and Co., 1863.

Hamilton, J. G. de Roulhac, ed. *The Papers of Randolph Abbott Shotwell.* 2 vols. Raleigh: North Carolina Historical Commission, 1929-1931.

Harris, William C., ed. *"In the Country of the Enemy": The Civil War Reports of a Massachusetts Corporal.* Tallahassee: University Press of Florida, 1999.

————. "Lincoln and Wartime Reconstruction in North Carolina, 1861-1863." *North Carolina Historical Review* 63 (April 1986): 149-168.

————. *William Woods Holden: Firebrand of North Carolina Politics.* Baton Rouge: Louisiana State University Press, 1987.

Hattaway, Herman, and Archer Jones. *How the North Won: A Military History of the Civil War.* Urbana: University of Illinois Press, 1983.

Henry, Robert S. *The Story of the Confederacy.* Indianapolis: Bobbs-Merrill Co., 1936.

Hurmence, Belinda, ed. *My Folks Don't Want Me To Talk About Slavery.* Winston-Salem: John F. Blair Publisher, 1984.

Johns, John E. "Wilmington during the Blockade." *Civil War Times Illustrated* 12 (June 1974): 34-44.

Johnson, R. U., and C. C. Buel, eds. *Battles and Leaders of the Civil War . . . Being for the Most Part Contributions by Union and Confederate Officers.* 4 vols. New York: Century Co., 1887-1888.

Johnston, Angus J. *Virginia Railroads in the Civil War.* Chapel Hill: University of North Carolina Press, 1961.

Johnston, Frontis W., and Joe A. Mobley, eds. *The Papers of Zebulon Baird Vance*. 2 vols. to date. Raleigh: Division of Archives and History, Department of Cultural Resources, 1963—.

Jones, Virgil C. *The Civil War at Sea*. 3 vols. New York: Holt, Rinehart, Winston, 1960-1962.

Jordan, Weymouth T., Jr., and Gerald W. Thomas. "Massacre at Plymouth: April 20, 1864." *North Carolina Historical Review* 72 (April 1995): 125-193.

Lefler, Hugh T., and Albert R. Newsome. *North Carolina: The History of a Southern State*. 3d. ed. Chapel Hill: University of North Carolina Press, 1973.

Luvaas, Jay. "Burnside's Roanoke Island Campaign." *Civil War Times Illustrated* 7 (December 1968): 4-11.

McClellan, George B. *McClellan's Own Story: The War for the Union, the Soldiers Who Fought It, the Civilians Who Directed It, and His Relation to It and Them*. New York: C. L. Webster and Co., 1887.

McPherson, James M. *Battle Cry of Freedom: The Civil War Era*. New York: Oxford University Press, 1988.

———. *Ordeal by Fire: The Civil War and Reconstruction*. New York: Knopf, 1982.

McWhiney, Grady, and Perry D. Jamieson. *Attack and Die: Civil War Military Tactics and the Southern Heritage*. Tuscaloosa, Ala.: University of Alabama Press, 1982.

Macartney, Clarence E. N. *Lincoln and His Generals*. Philadelphia: Dorrance and Co., 1925.

Mallison, Fred M. *The Civil War on the Outer Banks: A History of the Late Rebellion along the Coast of North Carolina from Carteret to Currituck*. Jefferson, N.C.: McFarland and Co., 1998.

Manarin, Louis H., ed. *Guide to Military Organizations and Installations in North Carolina, 1861-1865*. Raleigh: North Carolina Centennial Commission, 1961.

Manarin, Louis H., and Weymouth T. Jordan Jr., comps. *North Carolina Troops, 1861-1865: A Roster*. 14 vols. to date. Raleigh: Division of Archives and History, Department of Cultural Resources, 1966—.

Marvel, William. *Burnside*. Chapel Hill: University of North Carolina Press, 1991.

Massey, Mary E. "The Confederate Refugees in North Carolina." *North Carolina Historical Review* 40 (spring 1963): 158-182.

Meade, Robert D. *Judah Benjamin and the American Civil War.* Chicago: n.p., 1944.

Merrill, James M. "The Hatteras Expedition, August, 1861." *North Carolina Historical Review* 29 (April 1952): 204-219.

"Minutes from the Meetings of the Soldiers' Relief Society of New Bern, N.C., September 1861 through 1862." Museum of the Confederacy, Richmond, Va.

Mobley, Joe A. *James City: A Black Community in North Carolina, 1863-1900.* Raleigh: Division of Archives and History, Department of Cultural Resources, 1981.

———. *Ship Ashore! The U.S. Lifesavers of Coastal North Carolina.* Raleigh: Division of Archives and History, Department of Cultural Resources, 1994.

Moore, Mark A. *Moore's Historical Guide to the Wilmington Campaign and the Battles for Fort Fisher.* Mason City, Iowa: Savas Publishing Co., 1999.

Nelson, B. H. "Some Aspects of Negro Life in North Carolina during the Civil War." *North Carolina Historical Review* 25 (April 1948): 143-166.

Nichols, Roy F., ed. "Fighting in North Carolina Waters." *North Carolina Historical Review* 40 (January 1963): 75-84.

Norris, David A. "'For the Benefit of Our Gallant Volunteers': North Carolina's State Medical Department and Civilian Volunteer Efforts, 1861-1862." *North Carolina Historical Review* 75 (July 1998): 296-326.

———. "'The Yankees Have Been Here!': The Story of Brig. Gen. Edward E. Potter's Raid on Greenville, Tarboro, and Rocky Mount, July 16-23." *North Carolina Historical Review* 73 (January 1996): 1-27.

Official Records of the Union and Confederate Navies in the War of the Rebellion. 30 vols. Washington, D.C.: Government Printing Office, 1894-1922.

Owsley, Frank L. *King Cotton Diplomacy: Foreign Relations of the Confederate States of America.* Chicago: University of Chicago Press, 1959.

Parker, William H. *Recollections of a Naval Officer, 1841-1865*. New York: Scribner's Sons, 1883.

Parramore, Thomas C. "The Burning of Winton in 1862." *North Carolina Historical Review* 39 (winter 1962): 18-31.

Peterson, Owen M. "W. W. Avery in the Democratic National Convention of 1860." *North Carolina Historical Review* 30 (October 1954): 463-478.

Poore, Benjamin P. *The Life and Public Services of Ambrose E. Burnside, Soldier, Citizen, Statesman*. Providence, R.I.: J. A. and R. A. Reid, 1882.

Powell, William S., ed. *Dictionary of North Carolina Biography*. 6 vols. Chapel Hill: University of North Carolina Press, 1979-1996.

Randall, J. G., and David Donald. *The Civil War and Reconstruction*. 2nd. ed. Lexington: Mass.: D. C. Heath, 1969.

Raper, Horace W. "William W. Holden and the Peace Movement in North Carolina." *North Carolina Historical Review* 31 (October 1954): 493-515.

Rawick, George P., ed. *The American Slave: A Composite Autobiography*. 19 vols. Westport Conn.: Greenwood Press, 1972-1977.

Reed, Rowena. *Combined Operations in the Civil War*. Annapolis: Naval Institute Press, 1978.

Reid, Richard. "Raising the African Brigade." *North Carolina Historical Review* 70 (July 1993): 266-297.

Richardson, James D., comp. *A Compilation of the Messages and Papers of the Confederacy, Including the Diplomatic Correspondence, 1861-1865*. Nashville: United States Publishing Co. 1905.

Robinson, William M. *The Confederate Privateers*. New Haven: Yale University Press, 1928.

Rose, Rebecca, ed. *Colours of the Gray: An Illustrated Index of Wartime Flags from the Museum of the Confederacy's Collection*. Richmond: Museum of the Confederacy, 1998.

Rowland, Kate, ed. "Letters of Major Thomas Rowland, C.S.A., from North Carolina, 1861-62." *William and Mary Quarterly Historical Magazine* 25 (October 1916): 73-74.

Sauers, Richard. *A Succession of Honorable Victories: The Burnside Expedition in North Carolina*. Dayton, Ohio.: Morningside House, 1996.

Scharf, John T. *History of the Confederate States Navy from Its Organization to the Surrender of Its Last Vessel.* New York: Rogers and Sherwood, 1887.

Singleton, William Henry. *Recollections of My Slavery Days.* Edited by Katherine Mellen Charron and David S. Cecelski. Raleigh: Division of Archives and History, Department of Cultural Resources, 1999.

Soley, James R. *The Blockade and the Cruisers.* New York: Scribner's Sons, 1883.

Spraggins, Tinsley L. "Mobilization of Negro Labor for the Department of Virginia and North Carolina, 1861-1865." *North Carolina Historical Review* 24 (April 1947): 160-197.

Stick, David. *The Outer Banks of North Carolina, 1584-1958.* Chapel Hill: University of North Carolina Press, 1958.

Still, William N., Jr., ed. *The Confederate Navy: The Ships, Men, and Organization, 1861-65.* Annapolis: Naval Institute Press, 1996.

Thomas, Gerald W. *Divided Allegiances: Bertie County during the Civil War.* Raleigh: Division of Archives and History, Department of Cultural Resources, 1996.

Thompson, Robert M., and Richard Wainwright, eds. *Confidential Correspondence of Gustavus Vasa Fox, Assistant Secretary of the Navy, 1861-1865.* 2 vols. New York: DeVinne Press, 1918-1919.

Trotter, William R. *Ironclads and Columbiads: The Civil War in North Carolina—The Coast.* Winston-Salem: John F. Blair Publisher, 1989.

Tucker, Glenn. *Zeb Vance: Champion of Personal Freedom.* Indianapolis: Bobbs-Merrill Co., 1965.

Turner, George E. *Victory Rode the Rails: The Strategic Place of the Railroads in the Civil War.* Indianapolis: Bobbs-Merrill, 1963.

Upton, Emory. *The Military Policy of the United States.* 1912; New York: Greenwood Press, 1968.

Vandiver, Frank E. *Ploughshares into Swords: Josiah Gorgas and Confederate Ordnance.* Austin: University of Texas Press, 1952.

War of the Rebellion, The: A Compilation of the Official Records of the Union and Confederate Armies. 70 vols. Washington: Government Printing Office, 1880-1901.

Weigley, Russell F. *The American Way of War: A History of United States Military Strategy and Policy.* New York: MacMillan Publishing Co., 1973.

Wise, Stephen R. *Lifeline of the Confederacy: Blockade Running during the Civil War.* Columbia: University of South Carolina Press, 1988.

Yates, Richard E. "Governor Vance and the End of the War in North Carolina." *North Carolina Historical Review* 18 (October 1941): 315-338.

Index

attacks Fort Fisher, in joint expedition with Navy, 136
controls little of North Carolina (1862), 85
drummer of, pictured, i
master plan of, to occupy North Carolina, 65–66
misses opportunity to advance into mainland North Carolina, 22
plans second invasion of coastal North Carolina, 23
presses Confederacy from north and west (1862), 121
soldier of, pictured, ii
soldiers of, attacking Fort Fisher, pictured, 140
supply center at Plymouth, 112
treats escaped slaves as freedmen, 92, 94
victory of, at Forts Clark and Hatteras, 14
Ashby's Harbor, N.C., 35–40
Astor, John J., 79
Atalanta (later *Tallahassee, Olustee*), 134
Atlantic and North Carolina Railroad
connects Goldsboro, Kinston, New Bern, and Morehead City, xxiv
Federal armored train patrols daily, 69
military activities involving, 49, 107–108, 145
Atlantic Blockading Squadron (*earlier* Coast Blockading Squadron), 6, 16. *See also* North Atlantic Blockading Squadron, South Atlantic Blockading Squadron
Atlantic Ocean, xix, xvii, xxi, 133
Atlantic seaboard, xv
Averasboro, N.C., 145

B
Bahamas, xv, 129
Ballast Point, 33
Baltimore, Md., 77
Bancroft, George, 79
Banshee
blockade-running by, xv–xviii, 131
crew of, xvi–xvii
pictured, xiv
Barrett, John G., 50, 67, 102
Barrington's Ferry, 107, 111
Barron, Samuel, 5, 12–13, 19
Barton, Seth M., 110–111
Batchelder's Creek, 111
Battery Buchanan, 141
Battery Worth, 113
Beasley, Mrs., 125

Beaufort, 5–6, 34
Beaufort County, N.C., 83, 96
Beaufort Inlet, xix, 4, 56
Beaufort, N.C., 128
blockade-running to and from, 64, 131
British officers visiting, call Fort Macon indefensible, 61
escaped slaves flee to, 93
freedmen's camp at, 106
harbor of, protected by Fort Macon, 60
military activities in or near, 16–17, 27, 56, 63, 111
port and transportation facilities of, xxi, xxiv–xxv
Beauregard, P. G. T., 116–117
Beckwith, Nannie, 125
Bell, John, 2–4
Bennett, James, 147
Bentonville, N.C., Battle of, 145–147
Bermuda, 131
Bertie County, N.C., 87
blacks. *See* African Americans
Black Warrior, 34
blockade, Federal naval, of the Confederacy
along Atlantic coast, 6
Banshee evades, xv–xviii
commerce raiders slip through, 134–135
designed to force Confederate submission, 23
difficulty of enforcing at Cape Fear, 133
extends through 3,500 miles of coastline, xxv
in Federal campaign to capture Fort Macon, 57
map of, 131
successes of, 131
blockaders, Federal naval. *See* blockade, Federal naval, of the Confederacy
blockade-runners, Confederate. *See* blockade-running, Confederate
blockade-running, Confederate
Federal forces capture two blockade-runners near Fort Macon, 64
through Hatteras Inlet, 6, 24
severely hampered by Federal success in coastal North Carolina, 67
to and from Wilmington, xv, xvi, xviii, xxv, 5, 64, 67, 81, 129–130
Blockade Strategy Board, 6, 23
Blount's Creek, 108
Bogue Banks, N.C.
Fort Macon at eastern tip of, 56
military activities on or near, 59, 63
at southern tip of Outer Banks, xix
Bogue Inlet, 16
Bogue Sound, xix

operates most hospitals in
North Carolina, 126
tax-in-kind law of, 121–122
largest earthworks in, at Fort Fisher, 136
last skirmishes in, 148
Lincoln's reelection ensures relentless
Federal warfare against, 130
lose last coastal stronghold when
Wilmington surrenders, 144
North Carolina joins, 1
North Carolina's military contributions
to, xxiii, 5–6
Outer Bankers seek to avoid military
service for, 79
port facilities of, at outset of
Civil War, xxv
pro-Unionism in, 75, 80
railways of, at onset of Civil War, xxiv
secession from the Union of, 4
secret agents of, 132
transportation facilities of, 49
See also South
Congress, Confederate States, 123, 126
Congress, United States
Charles Henry Foster claims election
to, 75, 78, 80–81
Edward Stanly elected to, 83
enacts liberation of escaped slaves who
reach Federal forces, 94
Connecticut, 28, 83, 85
Conner, Mary Jane, pictured, 99
Conservative Party, 85, 121, 123
Constitution, Confederate States of
America, 4
Constitution, United States, 2, 34, 96
Constitutional Union Party, 2
"contrabands," 92–98, 104–105, 109, 112
pictured, 93–98
See also African Americans
Conway, T. W., 79
Cooke, James W., 113, 115
Cooper Institute, 79–80
Core Sound, xix
Cossack, 29
Cotton Plant, 34, 117
Cox, Jacob D., 143, 145
Craven County, N.C., 102
escaped slaves from outside, flee to
New Bern in, 93
plantation owners of, support
Democratic Party, 1
possesses ironworks, xxiii
voters of, support calling secession
convention, 4
Croatan Sound, xix, 34–35, 37–38
Croatan Works, 51

Crossan, Thomas M., 5, 133–134
Cumberland, 9
Curlew, 19, 34, 38
Currituck Canal. See Albemarle and
Chesapeake Canal
Currituck County, N.C., 2–4
Currituck, N.C., 42
Currituck Sound, xix, xxi
Cushing, William B., 70, 117–119
pictured, 118

D
Dahlgren howitzer, 39
Daily Progress (New Bern, N.C.), 127
Daniel, Junius, 107
Davis, Charles H., 23
Davis, Jefferson
authorizes discussion of suspension
of hostilities, 147
declines to assign troops in Virginia
to North Carolina, 32–33
distrusts loyalty of North Carolina to
Confederacy, 32–33, 55, 110, 116, 122
helps restore calm in Raleigh, 123
Lee seeks approval of, for attempt
to capture New Bern, 110
Lee warns, of possible disaster in
North Carolina, 55
promotes Robert F. Hoke to major
general, 116
Davis, Nannie, 126
Dawson, John, 144
Day Book (Norfolk, Va.), 77
Daylight, 133
Dearing, James, 111
Deep Gully, N.C., 93, 107
Delaware
in Federal campaign against Roanoke
Island, 29, 38, 40
in Federal capture of New Bern, 50
in Federal capture of Washington,
N.C., 65
in Federal seizure of Winton, 47–48
Democratic Party
national, 1–2, 77
of North Carolina, 1–2, 122
northern faction of, 2
southern faction of, 2, 77
Democrats. *See* Democratic Party
Department of the East (U.S.), 27–28
Department of the Navy, United States, 133
Department of Norfolk (C.S.A.), 33
Department of North Carolina (C.S.A.),
32–33, 55, 110

relies upon supplies from Wilmington, 131–132

surrenders at Appomattox, 91, 147–148

Lenapee, pictured, 141

Lewis, Mrs. Julius, 128

Liberator, 2

Lifesaving Service, United States, 102

Liles, Tempie, 43

Lillian, pictured, 134

Lincoln, Abraham

appoints Edward Stanly military governor of North Carolina, 81, 83, 97

approves invasion of coastal North Carolina, 25

becomes convinced that slavery must be eradicated in United States, 106

believes majority of Southerners remain loyal to Union, 75

Charles Henry Foster seeks to meet, 78

considers invasion of coastal North Carolina impractical, 23

considers North Carolina ready for reconstruction (1862), 84–86

election to presidency triggers Southern secession, 2–4

forbids return of escaped slaves to rebels, 94, 98, 103

orders blockade of seaports in six seceded states, xxv

orders Burnside to join McClellan in Virginia, 67

re-election to presidency, 130

requested to reinforce Fort Hatteras, N.C., 24

seeks to restore North Carolina to Union, 25–26, 75–77, 80

Little Creek, 70

Liverpool, England, xxv

Lockwood, 30, 50

Longstreet, James, 107–108

Lord Clyde (later *Advance*), 133–134

Lost Cause, 124

Louisiana, 4, 75

Louisiana

in Federal campaign to take Cape Hatteras, 29–30

in Federal campaign to take New Bern, 50

in Federal defenses of Washington, N.C., 71, 108

lands at Washington, N.C., 65

Lowthrop Hall, 126

Lynch, William F.

commands Mosquito Fleet at Battle of Roanoke Island, 34–38, 42

commands North Carolina's naval forces, 19

pessimistic about fighting ability of North Carolina volunteers, 45

M

Maine, 77

Mallory, Stephen R., 32, 119

Manassas, 34

Manassas, Va., 33

Mann, Dr., 114–115

Mansfield, Joseph K. F., 22–24

Maria Pike, 29

Marine Hospital, 79

Martha Greenwood, 29

Martin, James G., 110–112

Martin, W. F., 11–13

Martin County, N.C., 67, 69

Mary Banks, 29

Maryland, 121

Mary Price, 61, 63–64

Massachusetts, 7, 28, 98, 103

Mattabesett, 117

Maxwell, J. G., 17

McClellan, George B.

directs Peninsula Campaign, 50, 65

orders Burnside to attack Goldsboro, N.C., 67

plans and directs amphibious assault on North Carolina coast, 23–25, 27, 49, 64

McCullock Rangers, 45

Meagher, Thomas F., 143

Means, James, 98, 103

Mecca, 93

Meekins, Mrs. A. M., 128

M-1832 Harper's Ferry muskets, 45

Mexican War, 1, 39, 45, 83

Miami, 113–114, 117

pictured, 115

Midgett's Hammock, 41

Miles, Nelson A., 91

Minnesota, 9–10, 12–13

Mississippi, xxv, 4

Mobile, AL, xxv

Monitor, xix

Monticello, 9–10, 16–17, 20

Moore, Mark A., 142

Morehead City, N.C.

connected to Goldsboro, Kinston, and New Bern by railroad, xxiv, 49

military activities at or near, 56, 59, 111–112

Morris, 29

Morse, 50

Mosquito, 34

"Mosquito Fleet," 34, 37, 42

in Federal seizure of Winton, N.C.,
47–48
occupies Plymouth, N.C., 66
Ninth Regiment New Jersey Infantry, 28,
30, 72
Nixon, Capt., 10–11
Norfolk, Va., 33, 42
construction of Confederate ironclads
in, 57
manufacturing facilities of, xxiii
newspapers of, 77
port facilities and shipping activity in,
xxi, xxv
threatened by Federal control of coastal
North Carolina, xxvi, 16, 25, 27, 47
two regiments of African Brigade
report to, 101
Norris, David A., 124
North
abolitionism in, 2, 97
sectional conflict with South, 77, 88
William Henry Singleton moves to, 102
North Atlantic Blockading Squadron, 6, 23,
26. *See also* Atlantic Blockading
Squadron
North Breaker Shoal, xviii
North Carolina
African Americans in, 86–106
antebellum economy of, xxi–xxiv
appended unofficially to Department of
Virginia (U.S.), 28
coastal, 22, xix–xxvi
African American women's activities
in, during Civil War, 127–128
blockade-running to and from,
xv–xvi, xviii
Confederate counterattacks (1863-
1864) in, 107–120
control of Cape Hatteras key to
Federal operations in, 16
effect upon Confederacy of Federal
presence in, 67, 75, 131–132
escaped slaves in, flee to and enlist
in Federal forces, 96, 98–99, 103
Federal congressional elections
(1863) held in, 85–86
first Federal invasion (1861) of,
5–22, 80
freedmen's camps in, 103–106,
127–129
Governor Vance alarmed by Federal
successes in, 65–66
inhabitants of, suffer both Federal
and Confederate impressment, 122
map of, xx
only two U.S. Navy ships guard
(May 1861), 133

pro- and anti-war feelings among
residents of (1864), 130
pro-Unionism in, 78–82, 121
role of women in, during Civil War,
123–129
second Federal invasion (1862) of,
23–46, 49
slavery in, 87, 89–91
state prepares to defend, 5–7, 32
votes to reelect Zebulon B. Vance
governor, 123
wayside hospitals in, 126
See also Rip Van Winkle State
Coastal Plain of, xxi, xxiii, 1, 66–67, 70,
73, 87
Confederate naval success in, 19
Confederates build ironclads in, 113, 119
dissatisfaction with Confederate
government in, 121–122
division regarding secession among
residents of, 1–4
eastern, 98, 109–110
end of the war in, 145–148
fall line of rivers in, xxi
Federal attempts to establish wartime
Unionist government in, 75–86
Federal naval blockade of, xxv
General Assembly of, xxiv, 4, 88–89
history of, xix
home front activities in, during the war,
121–130
House of Commons of, 83
included within Federal government's
Department of the East, 27–28
mainland
coastal inhabitants flee to, 85
Confederate soldiers escape to, after
Battle of Roanoke Island, 42
farming on, 87
Federal forces lack foothold on
(1861), 75
Foster directs Federal raids into,
69–74
geography of, xix, xxi
successful Federal invasion of, led by
Burnside, 47–68
vulnerability of, if Federal forces
control coastal North Carolina,
xxvi, 22, 27
Medical Department of, 125
navy of, 5–6, 19
Piedmont of, 87, 123
pro-Unionism among residents of, 1–4,
18, 20, 25–26, 47, 65–66, 75–86, 98,
101, 121, 123
secession conventions (1861) of, 4, 77
secession of, from the Union, 1–4

Roanoke, 6
Roanoke Island Colony, 103, 105
Roanoke Island, N.C., 19
  Battle of, 37–45, 126
    map of, 37
  Confederate forces prepare to defend,
    32–34
  Confederate forces retreat to, 16, 21
  Confederate prisoners on, pictured, 43
  escaped slaves on, 92–93, 96, 102
  exaggerated reports of Confederate
    troop strength on, 18
  farming on, 87
  Federal forces invade and capture, xxvi,
    27, 32, 34–48, 51, 64, 66, 91, 103–104
  Federal forces use as base, 48, 57, 94
  freedmen's camp on, 105–106
Roanoke River
  flows into Albemarle Sound, xix, 117
  military activities on or near, 66, 69–70,
    113, 117
  Plymouth at mouth of, 112
Roanoke Sound, xix, 19, 41
Robertson, Beverly H., 107
Robeson County, N.C., 81
Robinson, Thomas, 35, 38
Roche, 29
Rocket, 29
Rocky Mount, N.C., 74, 108
Rogers, Hattie, 93
Rowan, Stephen C.
  assumes command of Federal naval
    forces in North Carolina, 50
  commands ships in campaign against
    Roanoke Island, 30, 38
  at Federal capture of Winton, N.C., 48
  orders naval expedition up the Roanoke
    River, 69
  orders naval force to protect
    pro-Unionists in Plymouth, N.C., 66
  reports extent of pro-Unionism in
    coastal North Carolina, 78
Rowan County, N.C., 2

S

Saint Augustine, Fla., xxv
Salisbury, N.C., 124
Sandfly, 34
San Francisco, Calif., 83
Sara Mills, 29
Sara Smith, 29
Sassacus, 117
Savannah, Ga., xxv
Schofield, John M., 142–143, 145–147
Scott, Winfield, 23–24
Scout, 29

Seabird, 29, 34–35
Second Battalion North Carolina Infantry,
  41–42, 45
  flag of Company A ("Brown Mountain
    Boys") of, pictured, 44
Second Brigade (U.S.), 28, 41, 49
Second Regiment Massachusetts Heavy
  Artillery, 112
Second Regiment North Carolina Colored
  Volunteers (*later* Thirty-sixth Regiment
  United States Colored Troops), 99, 102
Second Regiment North Carolina Union
  Volunteers, 81–82, 112, 115
Second Regiment United States Artillery,
  9–10
Second U.S. Congressional District of North
  Carolina, 80
Seddon, James A., 66
Sentinel, 29
Seven Days Campaign, 67
Seven Pines, Battle of, 67
Seventeenth Regiment Massachusetts
  Infantry, 69
Seventeenth Regiment North Carolina
  Troops (First Organization), 7, 12
Seventeenth Regiment North Carolina
  Troops (Second Organization), 71
Seventh Regiment North Carolina Troops,
  53
Seward, William L., 83
Seymour, 30
Shackleford Banks, 61
Shaw, Henry M., 34, 37, 39, 42–43
Shawseen, 30
Sherman, William T., 105, 142–143, 145–147
Shrapnel, 29
Singleton, Spier, 79
Singleton, William Henry, 102–103
  pictured, 100
Sixth Regiment New Hampshire Infantry,
  28, 57
Skirmisher, 29
slavery. *See also* "peculiar institution"
  abolition of, 85–86, 94–98, 106
  in coastal North Carolina, 89–91
  Confederacy defends continuance of,
    1–2, 121
  flourishes amidst large-scale agriculture,
    87
  South fears Federal government might
    abolish, 1–4, 88, 121
slaves. *See* African Americans,
  contrabands, slavery
Slocum Creek, 51
Smithfield, 71

White, Moses J., 59, 61–64
White, 42
Whitehall, 30
Whitehall, N.C., 72–73
Whitehead, 113, 117
White Oak River, 93
Whiting, William H. C., 110, 136, 138–139, 141
Wiard gun, 37
Wild, Edward A., xxvi, 99–102
Wild Rover, xxv
Wilkes County, N.C., 123
William Crocker, 29
William Putnam, 30
Williams, William T., 47
Williamston, N.C., 66, 70
Wilmington, 119
Wilmington and Manchester Railroad, xxiv
Wilmington and Weldon Railroad
  begins operating (1840), xxiv
  essential to supplying Confederate forces in Virginia, xxvi, 25, 131
  hospitals located near, 125–126
  military activities involving, 27, 71–74, 109
Wilmington, Charlotte, and Rutherfordton Railroad, xxiv
Wilmington, N.C., 88, 125
  blockade-running to and from, xv–xvi, xviii, 5, 64–65, 81, 131–134
  Burnside's long-range plan to capture, 56
  Confederate commerce raiders operate from, 134–135
  Confederate forces at, commanded by Joseph P. Anderson, 33
  Confederate hospital in, 126
  essential to supplying Confederacy, 131–132
  Federal campaign captures, 135–145
  Federal troops from, join Sherman's forces at Goldsboro, 147
  headquarters of Department of North Carolina and Southern Virginia (C.S.A.), 110
  ironclad construction at, 119
  map of, 133
  military activities in or near, xxvi, 4, 27
  North Carolina's only deep-water port during Civil War, xix–xx
  pictured, 143
  railroad links to its port, xxiv–xxvi
  Samuel G. French takes command of Confederate forces defending, 55
  sizable free African American population of, 87

yellow fever epidemic (1862) at, 129–130
Windsor, N.C., 66
Winslow, 5–7, 12–13, 34
Winton, N.C., Federal forces seize, 47–49
Wise, Henry A., 33–34, 37, 42, 45
Wise, O. J., 41
Wise's Forks, Battle of, 145
Wood, John Taylor, 110–112, 134
Wool, John
  commands Department of Virginia, 28
  commands Fort Monroe, Va., 9, 17
  receives report on pro-Unionism in coastal N.C., 28
  relieves Rush Hawkins of command of Cape Hatteras garrison, 21–24
Worcester, Mass., 103
Works Progress Administration, United States, 89
Wright, A. R., 19, 34, 57–58
Wyalusing, 117

Y
YMCA, New York, 96
York River, 65
Yorktown, Va., 65

Z
Zouave, 29–30
Zouaves. *See* Ninth New York Regiment, New York Infantry (Zouaves)